3-

FORMATION OFFICE

SPIRITUAL JOURNEYING

Spiritual Journeying

Directions on the Path for Prayer

by

Mary R. Prose, CHS

VANTAGE PRESS
New York / Washington / Atlanta
Los Angeles / Chicago

FIRST EDITION

*All rights reserved, including the right of
reproduction in whole or in part in any form.*

Copyright © 1980 by Mary R. Prose, CHS

Published by Vantage Press, Inc.
516 West 34th Street, New York, New York 10001

Manufactured in the United States of America
ISBN: 533-04472-3

Library of Congress Catalog Card No.: 79-67513

To all who have asked the questions
I am trying to answer,
especially John K., Pablo, Kris and John B.,
Maria and Lee, Carol, and Helen,
who not only questioned
but also challenged

Acknowledgments

Grateful acknowledgment is extended to the publishers and to others holding copyrights who have given me permission to quote from copyrighted materials. These include the National Council of the Churches of Christ in the United States of America for permission to use excerpts from the Revised Standard Version of the Bible, copyrighted 1946, 1952, © 1971, 1973, and from the Revised Standard Version Apocrypha, copyrighted © 1957, to Harcourt Brace Jovanovich, Inc., for permission to quote from T. S. Eliot's poems "The Waste Land," "The Love Song of J. Alfred Prufrock," and "Gerontion" in *The Complete Poems and Plays* © 1930–1962; to The University of Chicago Press and to John Frederick Nims for permission to use parts of his translation of the poems of St. John of the Cross.

In addition, I wish to express my appreciation to the editors of Vantage Press for their sensitive handling of my materials and to the supporting departments for making this venture in publishing an easy and pleasant one for me.

My gratitude goes also to my religious family, The Community of the Holy Spirit, for encouragement and support while I was working on this book, and to Kris and John Bomben, Sue and Doug Goodell, Dawn and Jerry Saunders, and Maria and Lee Shahinian for providing the solitude I needed for extended stretches of writing. I include here a word of thanks to Tom Davis for perceptive observations concerning parts of the manuscript, and to all others whose suggestions and experiences have enriched my work.

Contents

Prologue

"How do you pray, Sister Mary?" Friends, and sometimes strangers, have been asking me this lately, often in baffled tones, always with the urgency of those who search. A divine force seems to be drawing many persons today on a spiritual journey, toward deeper communication with the Source of their being. In response to their plea for help a multitude of methods and systems have surged forward: Zen, yoga, transcendental meditation, Pentecostal prayer, Scriptural prayer, creative liturgies, all in many varieties. To the degree that these modes deepen, expand, advance the religious awareness of those who practice them, they are good. Some persons pass from one to the other, seeking to satisfy different religious needs. Some settle in the framework of one system, sometimes because it satisfies their needs, sometimes because it provides a certain security. Some, poised on the edge of a system, seem to operate on a superficial level, afraid of the change and risk involved in growth. And many, turning away from procedures that seem complicated or uncongenial, continue to long for an acceptable relationship in prayer with their Creator.

To this last group, this little book chiefly presents itself . . . to those who are looking for simple, direct prayer, free from as many structures and trappings as possible. A prayer that is their own and God's, open to all the nuances emerging from their individual uniqueness and from the inexhaustible riches of the Being with whom they seek communication. The reason they desire to pray is not directly connected with adoration, reconciliation, thanksgiving, petition —although all these will inevitably be woven into their prayers. They are looking for a loving relationship with him who conceived the idea of them, individually and personally, and brought them individually and personally into being because he loved that idea.

There is more than one direction prayer can take. Prayer is communication, mutual exchange, with God. Communicating takes place in many ways: through spoken words or by signs, through reasoned discourse or by intuition, through learning or by experiencing, through doing or by being. Too often prayer has been confined to the oral formulas learned in childhood. To mature in prayer means to explore all possible means of communication with God.

Some of the directions in which we may go on this spiritual journey of exploration in prayer will be suggested in the pages that follow.

SPIRITUAL JOURNEYING

CHAPTER 1

Listening and Responding to God's Voice in Nature

To want to go on a spiritual journey at all, one must be aware in some degree of the lovableness of God, to whom the journey leads. This awareness will awaken a love for him. To begin to love God, one must begin to know him. Almost always a person reaches the maturity possible for love, burdened with a distorted concept of God, partly handed down by our culture and partly the result of childish and limited putting together of all the ideas received about God as one is growing up. To begin to know God in order to love him, one must rid oneself of the image or images man has made of God in the likeness of *man*: that of autocratic tyrant, of superpoliceman and detective, of Santa Claus, of one's own father. One must also wrestle with more sophisticated ideas, e.g., that God is a nonpersonal ruling Energy or Force or Design.

How can one begin to know what God is like? Perhaps the first move would be to increase awareness that God is communicating what he is like to us all the time, in every aspect of creation. Every sunset, every linnet's warble, every jasmine's perfume, every cherry's tang is a *word* of God telling us something about himself. God's words revealing himself are his creations. He speaks stars, mountains, seagulls, and apple blossoms. His beauty, his power, his inventiveness con-

1

cretize themselves before us every minute of the day. Who but God could have conceived the idea of a spider web sparkling with dewdrops? Of a rollicking kitten? Of explosive force compressed in the minuteness of the invisible atom? I open wide my eyes and ears and all my senses to drink in his ever-unrolling revelation of his beauty, his strength, his creativeness.

And what of his goodness and his love? These are the qualities of God I want most to know about and experience. With what words does he communicate to me that he is love and goodness? With the warm, living human words who are the persons in my life. Those who took care of me in my helpless babyhood; those who believe in me, shared with me, inspired my admiration. In other words, I have learned what goodness and love are from human beings who have been good to me and have loved me. And I have understood what love is by experiencing in myself burning, breath-catching love for others, and the peace and joy that come when I realize I am loved. I know that this goodness and love must be in God, or it could not appear in these things of his creation. He speaks through them to me, and I understand better what he is like.

And so I begin with simple knowledge of God in his beauty, power, creativeness, goodness, and love. I begin to relate to and love this being who reveals himself to me. Pondering these words of his in my heart, I listen for more. I try to become quiet within myself so that I can hear better. I concentrate upon becoming aware of his presence and growing familiar with his voice. In my hushed listening, each component of creation within my small sphere becomes a personal, pulsating word to me from him, who first had the idea of me, loved that idea of me, brought me into being, and in his love communicates with me in his own language—the words of nature, inanimate, animate, and personal. I keep wanting to expand and deepen my little sphere so that I can learn more and more about him.

But then a doubt insinuates itself into this growing relationship. To believe that God is communicating his love for *me* appears fantastic. How can I be sure that he loves me? The answer to that question gradually seems quite obvious: I *am;* therefore God loves me. Aware of his power and inventiveness, I am convinced that he would not have created me if he had not loved the idea of me. Who could have made him create me? He must have *wanted me.* And conscious through human experience of what love can be, I am overwhelmed with the realization of what love of God, the source of all love, must mean. I must not be niggardly in my concept of his love, reducing him to my own little human limits. I must become intensely conscious of the greatest possibilities of human love; and then, aware that this is only a minute model of God's love, multiply it in my mind in all its human aspects and components an infinite number of times. There can be no doubt of God; he is not subject to the fickleness and misunderstandings of human beings, limited as they are. The flaws of created beings help to point up the fullness of being in the ultimate creator whom I call God. And so I am grounded on unshakable security in the certainty of his fidelity, his complete understanding of me, his care, and his caring.

But what is God saying to me through the destructive forces of nature, and through decay, disease, death? No doubt, he is deepening my understanding that the elements in which these exist are not God. I do not always understand his mode of relating with me and with the rest of his creation. But then I must take care not to reduce him in my mind to my own puny powers of knowing and doing. He is enfleshed in every particle and aspect of the cosmos, but he is much more than that. I cannot box him into the scientific method nor any other category of my limited reasoning. Mystery confronts me on the outer edges of the cosmos. But the cosmos is within this mystery, an integral part of it. I cannot tell God how to run his world. He sees the whole design, I only a fragment. Faced by the aspects of his complete knowledge, his goodness, his love, and his power, I trust him to bring out of these seeming evils ultimate good.[1]

CHAPTER 2

Listening and Responding to God's Voice in People

People are, of course, part of God's creation, the crowning point. But because of the freedom he has given his people, we become to each other a very complicated expression of him in our spiritual journeyings. Although the goodness and beauty and giftedness of human persons are potent words revealing God to us, we are confounded and confused by the problems of evil and suffering present in all of humankind. It is difficult, with our myopic spiritual vision, to find our way on our path to God through the obfuscation of hate, envy, treachery, and violence. Here is where another source of communication with our Creator becomes a means of clarification: the recorded religious insights of the evolving human race.

In the Hebrew book of *Genesis,* these significant words occur:

Then God said: Let us make man in our image, after our likeness, and let them have *dominion* over the fish of the sea, and over the birds of the air, and over the cattle, and over all the earth . . . So God *created man in his own image,* in the image of God he created him;

4

male and female he created them. And God blessed them, and God said to them, "Be fruitful and multiply, and fill the earth and subdue it."[1]

What is fully meant by *God created man in his own image* is possibly beyond our human comprehension. But when we consider the qualities that distinguish us from the rest of the creation we know, there are indications of what this image and likeness must be mirroring: the potential to reflect, reason, choose, will, love. God surely does not play deceitful games with us. If he has created us with the potential to reflect, reason, choose, will, and love, then he expects us to develop these potentials. If he sent our forebears out to have *dominion* over his rich creation and to subdue it, then he meant that all these potentials be exercised in discovering and using the treasures and powers his inexhaustible genius had implanted in the universe.

Human beings have, indeed, explored and discovered and put to use and re-created in new forms, and thus have developed in an astounding way. Their vision, however, is limited and their developed powers weak. There have been innumerable failures and breakdowns. After all, although made in his image, human beings are not God. Nevertheless, God has respected the freedom of choice and action with which he has endowed them. He has rarely intervened in a global way. Through prayer, however, he has constantly given to individuals insights as to how the mistakes could be avoided, tragedies rectified, and energies directed to the happiest interests of his people. He has all but compelled those who have listened to him in prayer—the prophets and mystics throughout the ages—to share their new understandings with the persons who touched their lives.

But always the free choice and action have been muddled by human ignorances, misunderstandings, weakness, and limitations. And over the centuries of evolution, false theories, failures, wrong uses of power, misdirection of energies have seemingly entrapped the human race. Evil and suffering abound because we have inherited centuries of interacting human weaknesses and ignorance. The state we are in shows us what happens when we try to isolate ourselves from God.

These evils and sufferings we need to try to remedy. It is to us that God has given the universe "to till and keep it."[2] When he looked over everything that he had made, he saw that "it was very good."[3] The crowning achievement of his creative action was the creature in his image and likeness, who had the ability to reflect and reason, the freedom to choose, and the will to act. This masterpiece would mature through the trials and errors of its evolutionary childhood and adolescence as a being who possesses God-like qualities but is not God.

Evil and suffering, then, are not God's doing; all that he created was "very good." Evil and suffering come from the reality that we who exercise the awesome God-like powers of reflecting and reasoning, freedom of choice and willing are simply not God. If we listen in prayer, he will counsel us, deepen our understanding, strengthen our initiative and courage, and renew us with His love. But the responsibility is ours; and he will not take back the gifts that make us truly human.

If we are really alive, we shall keep ourselves aware of where our world is and take on our share of responsibility for its positive direction and development. Prayer presupposes involvement. Jesus explicitly said this:

> Come . . . I was hungry and you gave me food, I was thirsty and you gave me drink, I was a stranger and you welcomed me, I was naked and you clothed me, I was sick and you visited me, I was in prison and you came to me. . . . Truly, I say to you, as you did it to one of the least of these my brethren you did it to me. . . . Depart from me . . . for I was hungry . . . thirsty . . . a stranger . . . naked . . . sick . . . and in prison . . . and you did not minister to me . . . as you did it not to one of the least of these, you did it not to me.[4]

6

The depth of our relationship with God, then, clearly depends upon our participation in solving the problems of his and our world. He opts before all to communicate with us through concrete contact with the suffering and deprived among his people, with whom he chooses to identify himself. "As you did it to one of the least of these my brethren you did it to me."

Not only do we need to share the basic material elements of human existence, but we need also to exchange ideas, insights, encouragement, and comfort with our contemporaries and peers. Such reciprocal give and take is a support to and an aspect of our prayer. The shared experiences of two, three, or more, surely make for a clarity and strength not found in those of one alone.

If two or three are gathered together in my name, there am I in the midst of them.[5]

In such community we can compare our reflections on the state of our times, on relevant ways and means to be applied for positive outcomes, on our own place and responsibilities. We can mutually confide our weaknesses, doubts, and fears. Opening ourselves to the communicating spirit of God, we can together seek out wisdom, assurance, and courage.

We meet God, then, in ministering to the needs of our fellow human beings. However, to acquire fullness and integrity of being as a human person entails more than narrow blind action. We are creatures who need to reflect, to dream, to explore in spirit, to get in touch with our unconscious, to analyze failures and weaknesses, to evaluate, to set priorities. For all this, we must allow each other space, quiet times with God in the heart of our being, touched by him, opening up to him, listening to him. His touch heals and gives growth; we must experience this ourselves and help bring this healing touch to others. He understands fully our doubts and questionings and needs. He will listen to his people. And in turn, we, all of us, must learn to listen as a people, fixing the eyes

7

of our spirit upon him that we may know what direction to take, attuning the ears of our soul to his wisdom, experiencing the expansion of our understanding and a new surge of courage—experiencing his love.

In my spiritual journey, then, I shall follow the direction of God's voice, calling to me through his people. The path will lead me in the light of the goodness, wisdom, beauty of persons in my world. It will also plunge me into darkness, the evil and suffering caused by others and by my own limitations. Needless to say, God will be with me in the struggle. The opportunity is there for an incredible intimacy with him to grow. And out of this teamwork with him will emerge, both in me and in others, matured human qualities. Unless I pursue this direction, the path of authentic prayer will be lost.

CHAPTER 3

Listening and Responding to God's Voice
in Myself

"God's glory is man/woman fully alive," wrote Irenaeus of Lyons. And my own God-given reason and feeling confirm this statement. If the Supreme Artist started a pattern of potentialities evolving that one day would become *me,* naturally his joy is fulfilled in my becoming fully what he had in mind. No prayer can equal the prayer of my responding freely to God by *becoming.*

As a human being I possess inherited, built-in propensities toward growth as a unique person. In the long course of my evolution, however, these dynamic forces, carried in the genes of all my ancestors, have collided with other evolving powers, some good, some of a dark and evil nature, and have been turned by these and redirected, intertwined, and combined in ever increasingly complex systems. I was finally born on this earth, experiencing the inner push and pull of these internal and external forces but ignorant of their composition, structure, and meaning. Moreover, I was born into an exterior world that met my unique inner dynamism head on. And I experienced these outer forces, also, in ignorance of their elements and meaning. With my birth began the interaction between these inner and outer powers from which *I* am gradually emerging, more or less knowing, understand-

9

ing, choosing or rejecting, taking in hand and putting it all together into *me*. It is frightening at times, exciting, often delightful, often painful.

Many of the powers involved in the struggle continue to prove too strong for me to manage, and I have to come to terms with them, hopefully with personal dignity and continued growth. Sad it is for me as a person if I give up the struggle and allow myself to be captured by either the outer or inner powers: outer by conformism, imitation, and the many other influences that threaten my integrity as a unique person; inner by selfishness, sensuality, lethargy, negativism, and so on. I may little by little lose whatever personhood I have attained and regress into a thing, an *it*. At best, I shall cease to grow, to become.

On the contrary, if I persevere in the combat, pushing back ignorance with ever new knowledge and insight, bolstering weakness with the surrounding support of my fellow human beings and of my Creator, I shall become more and more fully alive in all the possibilities within me. The more fully alive I am as the person God has created me to be, the more vibrant, meaningful, and encompassing will be my relationship with him as well as with the human beings in my life.

Concerning my potentialities, that is, the complex inherited forces within me, and concerning the outer world into which I was born, I have no choice. I came into a world at a given time, a world shaped by evolution and history, possessing within myself unknown potentialities, an inherited constitution and drives, which I may gradually discover throughout the course of my life. I do have a choice, however, as to what attitude I shall take toward this world and toward myself. Do I choose to let these forces manipulate me, conforming myself to their pressures, succumbing helplessly and losing myself? Or do I choose to explore these mysteries, keep on uncovering their secrets, and apply them to my own growth as a person and to the development of the earth on which I find myself and of the society in which I live?

As to the world around me, I can set myself, to the degree circumstances permit, to master the accumulated knowledge derived from the experience and thinking of the human race preceding me. Examining this knowledge thoughtfully and realistically, I can reject what is useless and harmful, make new applications of the rest to the world of my own times, even going beyond with new discovering, experiencing, and improving. Thus I can affect the well-being of the world to some small degree, even to a considerable degree if I can unite my efforts with those of other like-minded people.

I know, by studying myself and other human beings, that God made me to be creative, fruitful, exercising initiative and responsibility; I find these potentialities in myself and others, and my reason confirms that God would not have devised them for nothing. I recall, too, the declaration in Genesis that God sent man and woman forth to till the earth and subdue it. Nothing positive and good that human beings have already accomplished in this task must be lost, and their mistakes and failures should warn and instruct us.

How are we to interpret "till and subdue" in the late twentieth century? Does it mean that we are to employ our highly developed technology for producing food, transportation, communication, and medical care to combat hunger and every other form of suffering wherever it is on the earth? Do we have an obligation to work at developing further what we already know about democracy and the dignity of the individual person, about economics, about cultures and social structures? Can we subdue the demons of war and greed and arrogant pride of power? If we make a conscious effort to direct our talents and energies toward such twentieth-century tilling and subduing, then we are communicating with God in a most authentic form of prayer. We are responding to him in concrete terms, telling him that out of love and gratitude we are struggling to overcome the adverse results of man's ignorance and weakness throughout history, struggling to propel the world in the direction he created it to go

—when, as recorded in Genesis, he looked at his creation and declared that it was *good*. Love is not expressed fully by words alone. Actions say more.

This much I know about my attitude toward the *outer* world in which I must grow and develop as a person. What about my *inner* world, my psyche, the spiritual element of me that bears within it my uniqueness, my potentialities: in other words, my sex, my special talents, my psychological drives, my inherited strengths and weaknesses, all of which seem to be imprinted upon my very biological structure? I need to explore them, to feel them as part of my person, to understand them, and to accept them as the real me, the single one of its kind. How unreasonable it is, even cruel, of my culture from babyhood on to place emphasis upon imitation, upon making me model myself upon others, upon encouraging hero worship, upon pressuring me to numberless conformities, instead of helping me discover my gifts and develop the richness of the unique composition of energies that through all of evolution and history have finally concentered in me. To be sure imitation is useful in learning some of the physical skills basic to human functioning, such as walking, speaking, or using tools. But to reward conformity and to punish originality and creativity and variety in thinking and in life-styles impoverishes both the individual and society.

If I am to "give glory" to God by becoming more and more alive in all aspects of my being, I must first of all accept myself in all my potentialities, *like* what I find it possible for me to be—not trying to be someone else. The goal is not to be better than others but to be fully what *I* am and can be. I need then to discover and develop what I am capable of —physically, intellectually, aesthetically, socially with regard to loving and interacting with other persons, spiritually with respect to my relationship with God. All of these aspects of my person are essential to the complete me. If I allow one or other to atrophy, then all are diminished, and I am less than a full person.

Then there is that mysterious part of me called by psy-

12

chologists the "unconscious." It is mysterious because we know so little about it as yet. There are many of our inner activities we do not fully understand: many of our desires, repugnances, fears, moods, drives. Then there is the whole area of what some psychologists call the "collective unconscious": the experience of evolution and history somehow embedded in our constitution as human beings and influencing our lives in ways we do not understand. The more of all this unconscious I uncover and make conscious, the better I shall understand the inner working of my personality and character, and the more control I can exercise over my growth as the full human being I am destined to become.

The knowledge of myself described here is not easy to acquire. But the Creator has gifted me with intelligence and with the wisdom of past generations, most of which has been recorded in books to which I have easy access. In addition, I must have a real desire to know myself and the patience to observe and ponder over, compare and analyze what I observe about myself and about the external world. I must also develop the courage to explore and experiment. How *alive* am I? How can I become more alive in more aspects of my being? The possibilities may be limited by my particular environment. But however considerable these limitation may be, the possibilities are still beyond measure. How many of us have thoroughly explored all the possibilities of our narrow little neighborhoods? Or, if we have done so, sought out different and perhaps richer fields in which to grow as persons?

Each new revealing contact with the world about me or with the mysteries of my inner self expands and enriches my personhood. If I desire to become fully all God has created me to be, both in my personal evolution and in the world he has given me to shape and develop, I need to discover and make active all the possibilities within myself. I need to keep trying to recognize God's words in all I see, hear, touch, and sense around me, responding to them in openness, with a concentrated effort to understand, and with a courageous surge forward to action.

All this deepens the character of my communication with God. Just as in a human relationship, the higher the qualities and personal endowments the partners bring to it, the more each one has to share in the relationship, so in my relationship with God. The richer I become in all my attributes of person, the deeper, more intimate, and more fulfilling will become my communication with him.

Becoming more and more fully alive in all the areas of potential that God has conceived of as converging and developing into the complete unique me—this very becoming *is* a continuing act of authentic prayer. It is listening to God's messages (my potentialities) that I discover within myself, and responding by doing all I can to actualize them. God glories in our aliveness. He delights in our teamwork with him. In his love for us, he wants us as his coworkers in our own destiny and that of the universe he has given us. Communicating with him on successive levels of maturity, as I grow more fully alive as the person God wants me to be, becomes an ever more exhilarating and fulfilling realization of prayer. It is a sure direction on the spiritual journey.

CHAPTER 4

Maintaining Progress on the Spiritual Journey

No one is born with a fully formed ability to pray. Like other human forms of communication—listening and speaking, reading and writing, music, art—prayer must be learned through inherited knowledge, practice, and persevering discipline. Although there are psychological and historical reasons for believing that each person is born with an instinctive drive toward God, this tendency must be fostered if it is to eventuate in prayer.

As we have already noted, prayer is mutual exchange. And although God, from the beginning of our lives, speaks out to us continuously in the multitudinous words of his creation, we have to learn slowly and often laboriously to recognize him, to listen, and to respond. We communicate joyously with persons in our lives, but only after we have gradually and stumblingly learned how. And as long as we live, our lessons in communication need to be expanded and perfected over and over as we mature in ever-advancing spirals.

The deeper the knowledge of each other two persons have, the easier mutual communication. The stronger the conviction that understanding and love exist, the readier the reciprocal flow of confidences. There is no question about *God's* knowledge, understanding, and love of each of us. The problem is *our* increasing knowledge and understanding and love of him.

15

The sources for this increase can never be exhausted. The sciences and the arts are the records of mankind's research into all aspects of creation, probing, as it were, into the workings of the mind of the Creator. Each new scientific discovery and artistic achievement advances our knowledge of God. The moments when we become conscious of this truth are in themselves moments of prayer. The unrolling pages of history reveal much to us about ourselves in our relationship with God—our successes and our failures. The insights of philosophy and of literature and of religion deepen our understanding, opening up to us the wisdom of humankind accumulated over the ages. This burgeoning knowledge stimulates our progress on our spiritual journey.

It is not enough, though, simply to absorb intellectually these new facets of knowledge.We must also feel them and identify with them. Over the years we can involve ourselves in a variety of the sciences and the arts; life is much too short to encompass all there is to learn. Our scientists and our artists present us with the fruits of their explorations. They do not create the elements. They only discover them, experiment with their interaction, regroup them, suggest their significance and uses. Prayer occurs when we give credit where credit is due, to the One who in his creative power brought forth these elements, energies seeded with all the potentials for blossoming into the myriad forms and forces that constitute the cosmos and unify life.

Human relationships in which we can share our spiritual experiences are vital in maintaining our progress on the spiritual journey. As we have seen, the social element in our nature is a basic one, and we need one another for support and encouragement.

There are times, though, when, like Jesus, we must go aside to pray—into adjoining deserts or mountains of our own finding or along the quiet shore of a stretch of sea.

. . . when you pray, go into your room and shut the door and pray to your Father who is in secret . . .[1]

16

Each day surely we can allow ourselves some brief moments of inner solitude, when stepping beyond duties and distractions, we can be conscious of God alone, we can touch him and be touched by him. Perhaps it will be when awakening in the morning, at an interval in work, in the quiet before sleep. But it can also be an inner concentration on God at the busiest of moments or places. It is not length of prayer that is important here. It is a deep intensity of awareness and sharing.

Longer periods of solitude with God are, however, indispensable at regular intervals, perhaps monthly, or at favorite seasons, or at least, once during the year. These must not be left to chance. They can be arranged at organized retreat or renewal centers, or simply included in one's regular calendar of activities as times alone, preferably away from the ordinary routine, perhaps close to nature in some aspect that lifts us out of our everyday selves.

Besides these disciplines that we strive to weave into the texture of our lives, extraordinary needs sometimes require extraordinary measures. Fluctuating as our psychological and spiritual growth usually is, there will be times when we find ourselves apathetic, sluggish, dry, uninspired. When we become aware of this state, we must take it vigorously in hand. As in the maintenance of any other valuable human skill, prayer will require review and updating in a setting of discipline. It is the unusual person who can alone lift him/herself out of these doldrums. Such a paralyzing season may require the exercise of some structured programs perchance never experienced before. Perhaps the rejuvenating factor may be a deeper study of Scripture; creative liturgies; Zen or its western counterparts; participation in some awareness-raising group, such as a human potential workshop; or ministering to basic human needs of others. Perhaps some serious new reading and thinking or some pertinent lectures and discussions. Maybe the shock treatment of a plunge into a different culture or life-style or unexplored area of human suffering. Or sometimes the need may simply be to lie fallow for a while until the substance of ourselves, exhausted by giving and activity, can restore and renew its natural resilience. Milton says, "He also serves who only stands and waits." If the motive in undertaking any of these or other alternatives is to enrich or restore our communication with God, then the very effort in itself is prayer.

Reflecting back over the pages read, we come to realize that prayer springs from many sources and under different aspects. What is the common factor? the essence? Whatever its source or aspect, prayer begins with a consciousness that God is present for dialogue with us. We listen and respond. His words to us may be his works in nature, the persons who influence our lives, the extant evidences of his interventions in human evolution, the awareness of his gifts within us, or his silent illumination in the core of our being. His words may have a joyful or suffering content, may rise out of good or evil. There is an old proverb: "God writes straight with crooked lines." Our words to him may be in human language, unspoken desires, efforts to carry out our responsibilities to his people, endeavors to become fully alive ourselves. Whatever his words, if we listen, and respond in whatever mode, prayer is happening. The rhythm is: consciousness of God's presence, listening, responding, listening, responding. . . . Thus the spiritual journey keeps progressing.

In the chapters that follow, we shall consider some ways of heightening our listening and responding.

CHAPTER 5

Mystical Prayer

In my spiritual journeying, God surrounds me, fills me, and is present *to me* always and everywhere, whether or not I am conscious of him. Created as I am, a self-aware, free-willing, and self-directing person, I must on my part be present *to God* if I am to develop a true and growing relationship with him. There must be a tangible point of contact from which I can proceed. This point of contact is the fountainhead of all that makes my life growth-directed and fruitful. It is the meeting place of my God and me where I can transcend all that holds me back from him and through which he comes for intimate, personal contact with me.

This point of contact has been the goal of the insatiable seekers after God as far back as history records. They have called its realization by descriptive names, often metaphorical —the Enlightenment, mystical union, spiritual marriage, *satori*—and the way to reach this goal is *penetrating prayer*, made free to pursue the consummation of love by ascesis, that is, self-discipline.

All of us are called to be mystics. The quality of our lives depends upon the facility we acquire to penetrate the multitudinous manifestations of God in our lives to find him alone, the Real, at the core of them all.

Meditation, contemplation, mystical prayer—whatever name one chooses to call it—came into my own life through the Western masters: St. Therese of Lisieux (in my early teens) and the Carmelite school; the *Imitation of Christ;* the German and the English mystics; and Dominican and Jesuit writers on prayer.

Occasionally, through literary works, I brushed briefly with Oriental modes of prayer. But it was not until students and counselees of the 1960s started to question me about Zen, Tao, Buddha, the Vedanta, yoga, that I began to wonder how these Eastern systems differed from or resembled Western approaches to God. Extensive reading of the Eastern religious classics and their commentators, conversations with native and Western adherents to these religions or philosophies, and occasional opportunities to participate in their sessions convinced me that there are many similarities and a few radical differences.

Although among the many Oriental sects there are numerous variations and polarizations, for the most part they are like the majority of Western religions in that they see a God-centered life as necessary and good, and they seek union with God through discipline.

The underlying philosophies and goals, however, are different. To most Orientals, Brahma, Dharmakaya, the Tao, or whatever name they may give to the all-pervading and encompassing spirit is impersonal and manifests itself in all created forms, which eventually lose themselves again in the One. Matter, an illusion and the source of suffering must be annihilated. Peace can be obtained only by the extinction of desires and identification with the One.

In contrast, to most religious persons of Western culture, God is personal. All created things are brought into being by God but are not to be identified with him. Matter is good, and human beings have received the specific task of discovering its potential and developing it. Growth and fulfillment outweigh peace as the goal. Union with God is sought but without loss of personal identity.

20

Some apparent differences between the Eastern and the Western approaches may be only semantic. Improved modes of travel and communication are making it possible for the East and West to share insights from their religious and spiritual heritages, each slowly exerting a balancing influence on the other. Moreover, a plurality of approaches is surely valid for the kaleidoscope of temperaments, cultural settings, experiences, and opportunities among the widely scattered segments of the human race and within the broad range of differences within one segment. As rapid transportation and cultural exchange draw all peoples of the world closer to becoming one, effort intensifies to uncover the origins and common elements of mankind's spiritual development. The research of Carl Jung in this area, to give one example, opens up vistas for exciting exploration and speculation.

In a consideration of the contributions of both Eastern and Western approaches to prayer, a clarification of terms used must continuously accompany the process. *Mysticism, meditation,* and *contemplation* are sometimes used synonymously and at other times with widely varying meanings and connotations. *Mysticism* usually refers to a transconceptual grasp of reality. It transcends our intellectual processes and arrives directly at the core of that which we seek to know, understand, or experience.

With Western writers, *meditation* is normally discursive and reflective; it is a predominantly intellectual examining of truths, hypotheses, and experiences, an examination in which we use our human faculties to advance us toward a truer knowledge of ourselves and a grasp of the divine. It leads to a stirring of the feelings of love, hope, trust, sorrow, or whatever emotions are relevant at the time, which in turn move the will to action. *Contemplation,* or what is sometimes termed "infused contemplation," according to most Western authors, transcends the human intellect, feeling, and senses. It must be God-initiated. We human beings are not capable of achieving it ourselves; we can only prepare for it. Eastern writers traditionally uses the one word *meditation* to include both of these concepts, with perhaps a slight shade of difference in meaning because the idea of the divine for most of them is impersonal rather than personal.

For readers who, like me, need to appraise the present by the past, I have appended to this book a sketch of the history of mysticism, indicating the vast literature the serious student of prayer may explore and making selected recommendations. For those who care to do so, this would be a good place to peruse the historical background to our subject. (See the appendix, page 71)

Knowing about prayer, however, and actually praying are quite different, though allied, experiences. While we are researching the evolution of mysticism and pondering over the masters of each age in history, we shall want to be *praying*. How does a person of the late twentieth century set up a practical prayer life, a prayer life that will withstand the confusion and noise and pressures of our world, and that will impregnate the praying person with a true sense of the Real and with a dynamism rooted in love for impact on that world? For me, the answer to that question involves seven or more steps or elements, some of them depending principally on me and some on God. Prayer is a two-way communing. These elements are:

1) Desire and determination to pray
2) An environment that promotes prayer
3) Discursive or reflective meditation
4) Prayer of quiet
5) Experiencing God's presence
6) God's part in prayer
7) Prayer of union

An eighth element may helpfully be considered here. To offset discouragement, it is important to be conscious that the experience of *waiting* is part of the process. No credence is to be given to the common idea that if God does not respond to prayer, it is because the one who prays is unworthy.

Prayer is often a long wrestling with God, as exemplified in the Hebrew Scriptures by Jacob and the angel.[1] What happens to me during the wrestling in the way of growth and expanded awareness may be the true response to my prayer. Unworthiness has nothing to do with the outcome. The more unworthy I am, the more I must cry out. Persistence is the key ingredient when the process seems barren.

The stages may not always progress in their order just given. As elements rather than steps, they may eventually intermingle, diminish or increase in importance, and even fuse into one. But to begin with, it seems useful, to me at least, to view these stages as some sort of direction into the Unknown.

Desire and Determination to Pray

First of all then, I must have a strong *desire* for a deep relationship with the Source of my being and the Loving One toward whom I am evolving. Research in this area gives me ample evidence to believe that a propulsion toward God is implanted in me as part of my nature as a human being.[2] The seed must be nurtured, however; and in the kind of world in which I live, its growth can easily be misdirected. I may need help to discover this desire and to learn how to make it grow in its true direction. This assistance may come from a wise spiritual director, from retreats, conferences, books and articles deepening my knowledge of God and of prayer, from contacts with others who pray, and from life experiences that force me to face my insufficiencies.

Along with this desire, I must summon up an invincible *determination* to overcome the difficulties that will block my way to prayer: difficulties of time and place, of physical and psychological fatigue, of weak powers of concentration, of the strong pull of the senses and emotions in diverse directions. In the beginning especially, the attraction of the unseen and unknown real yields easily to the tug of the senses toward the concrete, colorful, touchable, audible components of the material world continuously brushing against me as it changes form and passes away. Perseverance may need the strengthening support of reasonable self-discipline and self-imposed structures. I emphasize *self,* since the loving relationship which prayer is can come about only by free choice.

An Environment That Promotes Prayer

In the beginning especially, and perhaps throughout life, an *environment conducive to prayer* is most helpful. When we have cultivated a strong habit of prayer, just to close the eyes and withdraw our energies to the core of our being suffices, no matter what the outer circumstances. This is possible in the midst of people, of noise, of ugliness, if we are deeply rooted in the realities of prayer. But if we are strange to the ways of prayer or suffering from dryness or desolation, a special *place* to which we may retire, a place of quiet with a touch of beauty and some meaningful reminder of God, makes it easier to slip past the obstacles of pleasurable distractions or of problem-solving, anxiety, bitterness, or self-pity. For different people, places of prayer will differ. For some it will be in awe-inspiring contacts with nature: under the freeing expanse of sky, star-filled, cloud-strewn, or blue and sunny; or by the mysterious sea; or from mountain heights, surveying the incredible vistas below; or surrounded by trees or flowers or rock formations; or facing rivers or lakes; or exulting in dawns or sunsets. For many people God speaks perceivably through the beauties of nature. For others the place may be a church or chapel, a simple home shrine, the aura of a moving work of art, or immersion in music that draws them to the divine. Or sometimes it may be in the presence of the poor, the sick, the dying. Individuals need to try out places until a convenient, prayer-promoting spot appeals. For some a variety may prove effective.

Environment is also affected by *time*. Some of us pray better in early morning, some in the evening. To secure aloneness and beauty, prayer time may need to be during the day or late at night. Each must discover what time works best in the given situation.

The optimum length of time for excellence in prayer must also be experimented with. Some persons meditate an hour in the morning and an hour at night, some a half hour, some twenty minutes. It is not the quantity but the quality that is important. Individual needs and abilities differ, and even the same person may vary in desire or requirement at different times of the year or at different phases in life.

Posture may be another determining environmental factor. Many Eastern religious groups prescribe the lotus position. Western Christians often kneel. Worshipers in some religions stand for prayer. Some prostrate themselves on the ground. Posture in itself is not particularly important, although the symbolic significance may stimulate the prayer of certain persons. Do we who pray meditate more effectively, communicate best with God, when prostrating, kneeling, sitting, standing, walking, or jogging? Each of us must determine the posture or combination of postures best suited to our temperament, personality, health, place, and circumstances.

My own preferences with regard to the environment for prayer have varied over the years. Although I can pray easily in almost any situation, nature in any quiet aspect—the sea, the mountains, the woods, the desert—is my most compelling setting. Since it is not always convenient to seek the out-of-doors for prayer, I choose most frequently the privacy of my room, sitting comfortably in a large chair in the warm atmosphere of my books and tokens of affection from significant people in my life. This environment arouses a sense of love, gratitude, and expansion of soul that carries me directly to God. Although evening is my favorite time, the usual activities of that period of my day make it necessary for me to structure an earlier hour, usually in the morning before I begin the work of the day. I do best with long periods; but again, the incursions of needful others make extended times of aloneness a luxury for me. I make up for this by brief soul movements inward to awareness of the presence of God at chance times during the day.

The question is sometimes asked: Is not the contact with God's people and God's world a continuous prayer? Yes, of course. But all my energies are so focused on what I am doing that usually I am not conscious of that kind of prayer except in retrospect. Sometimes I am able to put myself and the person or persons with whom I am working intensely in the presence of God, so that light, strength, and wisdom will increase in us. But usually my human limitations keep me during times of work or recreation from realizing God's constant presence.

"How do you use this time? What method do you follow? Do you reflect on Scripture? Practice breathing? Chant? Recite?" These queries have been put to me. I do all of these things at one time or another, and some rather consistently. They are means to and not the essence of prayer. Deep, conscious breathing is an effective aid to the relaxation that should precede prayer. Chanting or reciting may help concentration, if that is a problem. During most of my religious life, chanting and reciting the Divine Office with the rest of the community in chapel was the principal prescribed mode of prayer. Even now on occasions I enjoy chanting the Office with others, although for me that is more of an aesthetic or social than a prayer experience. I like to read the Divine Office slowly, stopping wherever I am moved to reflect on or savor the passage. The breviary has a great deal of variety as it follows the liturgical seasons and hours of the day. Since the Office is Scripture-oriented, it provides me with a broad selection of the sacred writings as food for prayer. However, at times I like to apply the same method to other passages of the Bible, to other books that connect me somehow to God, and especially to poetry. My most valued mode of prayer, though, occurs when I can pass beyond the written or spoken word to be simply present to God and united with him.

Another preparation for prayer is ascesis, or discipline. Most of the Eastern mystics stress ascetic practices, such as

26

fasting and diet, disciplined control of body, deprivation of rest, suppression of sense activity. Western and Middle Eastern mystics, the desert hermits, many of the monks, nuns, and other religious persons of the early Christian era, the Middle Ages, and the Renaissance also emphasized these ascetic elements, sometimes to the point that they seem an end in themselves rather than means to closer communion with God. In the West and to some extent in the East the result has been a reaction against these practices. In contemporary times each of us must recognize the need for some self-imposed structure and personal discipline to achieve a life of union with God.

With our fuller knowledge of the roles of the subconscious and unconscious, of the evolution of such psychological phenomena as suggestion, hypnosis, extrasensory perception, of the astounding discoveries by modern physics of intracosmic and transcosmic influences, modern mysticism can begin to distinguish between what is real and what is spurious, between what is necessary and what is useless baggage. Our growing knowledge of the sub- and unconscious shows us that we can move a considerable distance beyond consciousness on what is still a human, though dimly explored, level. Somewhere at the remotest edge of the unconscious we meet with the Transcendent. *Edge* here does not refer to space but to human experience.

As human persons motivated by love and by meaning, operating fully only at the level of free choice and willing, each of us strains more or less, according to the degree of human development in which we find ourselves, to determine our values, to give priorities to them, to realize them. Hopefully we discover the need of divine assistance to achieve the fullness of our potentialities. But along with this realization we become aware of the effort we ourselves are destined to put into the achievement. We have not been given bodies, minds, emotions, wills, and spiritual intuitions for nothing. Here ascesis or discipline becomes meaningful and desirable.

Normally, healthy bodies form the foundation for human structures better than unhealthy ones. The discipline of diet and exercise, of proper breathing and cleansing, are important here. Oriental Hatha Yoga with its training for flexibility of all parts of the body, its breathing control, its dietary and cleansing customs, has much to teach us Westerners, although few of us would wish to carry it to its extremes.

The development of our minds requires the discipline of time structures, of concentration, and of perseverance. The control and refinement of our emotions entails a delicate discipline that is positive rather than repressive. Our wills are strengthened by practice in initiating activities, facing difficulties, carrying through.

All this physical and psychological training puts us as human beings approaching wholeness in a condition to pursue with hope and steadfastness our spiritual intuitions. In contemporary spirituality, then, such ascetic practices become meaningful disciplines for strengthening our advance toward mystical union with God in prayer.

Discursive or Reflective Meditation

With our physical, psychological, and spiritual faculties disciplined for action, we turn to creating a prayerful atmosphere in which we can listen for God's response to our reaching out to Him. This usually has to be a gradual process. It may be achieved by *discursive or reflective meditation* in which we slowly read the Scriptures or some other appropriate book, or repeat a short prayer or aphorism or mantra, or recite a longer prayer thoughtfully with pauses, using the parts in all these cases as pegs on which to fasten our reflective prayer. This is part of the process for centering our prayer.

Prayer of Quiet; Experiencing God's Presence

Discursive meditation and reflective prayer may lead to what is called the *prayer of quiet,* a state of listening to God, an awareness of his presence as of that of a loved one in the dark. At this point, thinking and effort are suspended and the presence of God is simply *experienced* and savored. It is God's turn to communicate with us; and his communication is not in words but in direct act. Simone Weil, a modern mystic, describes this experience in these words:

> A presence more personal, more certain and more real than that of a human being. . . . I only felt in the midst of my suffering the presence of love, like that which one can read in the smile on a beloved face.[3]

God's Part in Prayer

God's touch is healing. Our ignorances are gradually suffused with understanding and wisdom; our apathy gradually converts into hope, joy, enthusiasm, and a momentum toward achievement; our anxieties give way to trust, openness, and peace; our coldness is fired by a mysterious love.

Prayer of Union

The mystical state may quickly disappear, although certain effects remain. But when it subsides from its peak to a steady and constant communion with God, we have entered into what is sometimes called the *prayer of union*. In this mystical way we find ourselves gifted with bursting energies transcending our natural abilities. Without straining, we see the unity of all creation and its dependence on God. Feeling our place in the universe, we are moved to follow the lead of the Spirit in "subduing" and "tilling"[4] our inheritance and cooperating in bringing to fruition the evolving plan of God's creation. In our concentration of our energy upon the task at hand, we may not always be *conscious* of our union with God. But it is easy to advert to him and to pass back and forth between awareness of him and the human limitation of needing to focus all of our faculties upon the here and now.

There is a peaceful assurance that he is lending his strength to our efforts.

It is important to remember that each school of mysticism rises out of a specific culture and point in evolution. Our search is principally for a mysticism that emerges naturally from *our* times and our vision. Since human nature has not changed radically, many of the mystical insights of the past are still valid. The world we live in, however, has changed. Our knowledge of it and our power over it have magnified beyond measure. Our comprehension of ourselves, biologically, psychologically, and sociologically, has expanded titanically in recent centuries, and glimpses of our potential for the future are staggering.

But then our limitations are staggering, too. With all that we know and can do, why do human beings suffer from poverty, from disease, from violence, from wars, from loneliness, from prejudice, from injustices in every form? What keeps us from taking on responsibility for ourselves, for one another, for our world, instead of shifting the blame for the mess we are in on any convenient scapegoat—even on God himself? Is it not conceivable that we can individually begin to right our relationship with our Creator and, in so doing, reach out to all members of our human family and assume responsibility for the earth we have been given to "till and subdue"? At the end of the twentieth century we need a fresh mysticism, not one to *escape* into to avoid the miseries we have created in our world, but one in which, by touching God, we can imbibe insight, strength, and invincible love to fulfill our part in evolving the world that God can look upon and see that it is good.

What can we gain then, in our contemporary reaching out for the Transcendent, by going back to the roots of mysticism? We can begin again to sacralize our world, seeing the divine impregnated in every part of it.[5] In the final analysis both Eastern and Western mysticism teach us this, although too often in both traditions the material aspects of creation are viewed as evil or illusory. It is not that the material ele-

30

ments of the world are in themselves bad—God looked at his creation and saw that "it was good"—it is what we human beings, in our ignorance, our pride, our selfishness, our weakness, do with them that produces evil. We must then see the divine in *all* of creation, treating it with reverence, assisting its potential for goodness, beauty, and beneficent power to develop, and sharing with one another, as stewards of God's bounty. We are not the owners, since we are not the creators, but only the discoverers and developers of the riches of the universe. The realization of this mystery comes to us through meditation and contemplation.

"By their fruits you shall know them."[6] The test of our prayer life is whether it promotes our growth as persons, making us more and more fully alive and responsible. The authentic fruits of mystical prayer are not ecstasy, aura, penetration of the future, visions, but love, trust in God, peace, hope, joy, compassion, truth, labor for the good of all others—in other words, *wholeness* as the human persons God created us to be.

CHAPTER 6

Scriptural Prayer

The deep thoughts and spiritual experiences of human beings throughout history are apt matter for reflective meditation and prayer, conveyed through any literary form whatsoever. Poetry, stories, drama, essays from many sources serve, as well as the sacred writings of the great world religions. The Hebrew and Christian Scriptures, however, have a significant role in Western civilization. They can be valuable in our prayer life in at least three ways: as a source of knowledge and deeper understanding of God and his manner of dealing with his people; as the script for discursive and reflective meditation; as a treasury of universal prayers that can be adapted to all persons and times. These values affect both personal and liturgical prayer.

The sacred writings are one dimension of God's revelation of himself to us. We may be sure that the better we know him and the more intimately we understand him, the more we shall love him and find joy in expressing that love in prayer. As the Vatican II Council document on *Divine Revelation* tells us: ". . . in the sacred books, the Father who is in heaven meets His children with great love and speaks with them."[1]

Because of the antiquity of the sacred texts, we need much help from scholars in deciphering their meaning and interpreting them, if our knowledge is to be more than superficial. A superficial knowledge, or a rigid, literal interpretation, can be misleading and even become a direct obstacle in the process of discerning God. Pius XII points this out in his significant encyclical on Scripture, *Divino Afflante Spiritu.* As summarized by a contemporary Scripture scholar, Pius XII's "fundamental postulate was that, if we are to understand the word of God, we must first know the spirit in which the word was written. We must go back to the ancient Near East—to its way of life, its mode of thinking, its manner of expression, including thought patterns and imagery—so that we can hear the word of God resonating in the time it was written. God's word is never an abstract word; it is always directed to the here-and-now, so much so that, unless this unchanging word is understood in the context of a specific time and place, its rich fullness is never known."[2]

In recent times, researchers in ancient languages, archaeologists, scholars developing adequate historical and literary criticism, have really opened up the treasures of the Bible to us. Numerous writers have translated their finds into readable forms for the nonexpert in these fields. (Some of the more helpful are listed in the Notes for this chapter.)[3] A little preparation for reading Holy Scripture and especially the use of reference materials will so enrich our study of the Bible that we shall more and more clearly see God revealing himself to us and clarifying the mysteries that surround our relationship with Him.

To know God is to love him, and to love him impels us to pray. Vatican II's *Divine Revelation* comments: ". . . prayer should accompany the reading of sacred Scripture, so God and man may talk together; for 'we speak to Him when we pray; we hear Him when we read the divine sayings.' "[4]

Discursive and reflective meditation has already emerged in this book as one of the stages toward mystical prayer. Of the myriad sources for such reflection, the Bible is surely the universal favorite in the West, both what we call the Old and New Testaments for Christians, and the Hebrew Scriptures for Jews. It is helpful to read the entire Bible, pondering it

33

slowly so as to get a feeling for the whole and to absorb its wisdom concerning both God and human beings. For prayer, however, certain passages have greater appeal than others and these can be marked for repeated reflection.

There is a depth and a height in the Scriptures that can carry us to ever-increasing rootedness and growth. Exploring certain parts on a given day may elicit an insight about God or about ourselves or others that prompts a response in prayer. After a lapse of time during which we meet with and engage in further reflection, the same passages can uncover fresh perspectives and wider horizons. As our understanding of God and of life increases, this same biblical theme can adapt itself in a multitude of ways to the stages and problems and circumstances of our human existence and leads us to richer prayer experience.

A specific application may help clarify these ideas. Having read the Old Testament, for example, I may become aware of God's having chosen, elected, a people to keep alive in his world the knowledge of its Creator and to manifest an ongoing relationship with him. I may be struck by the promises made to this people and by God's expectations of them; the covenant they entered into with God; their repeated failures and God's recurrent intervention to set them right; their vicissitudes in building their kingdom; their hopes for the future; the gradual refinement of their concept of God. Perhaps this insight will lead me to prayer of thanksgiving to God for his solicitude through the ages in keeping the knowledge of himself alive and constantly maturing among human beings.

A later meditation on this same subject may bring out the mystery of the human race's preparation for Christ and its call to become the *new* people of God. Reflecting on this thought may open up to my understanding how the Old Testament points to the New. The gospel of Matthew refers repeatedly to such signs and prophecies and so does Paul in some of his epistles. I may see the history of Israel reenacted in Christian history: the election; the new covenant; the vicissitudes of the new kingdom; the schisms, relapse, exiles;

34

the saving action of Christ, and the guidance of the Holy Spirit. My view of God's relationship with his world may be expanded and deepened, and this fresh insight may overflow into prayer of trust and hope and loyalty.

In a subsequent reflection I may discern the history of Israel in my own life: *my* election and vocation; the promises I understood God making to me and my promises to him; my vicissitudes in my progress through life—my defeats, exiles, desert experiences; God's faithfulness in supporting me and opening my soul to ever greater awareness of all he is to me. At this point, heightened understanding and deep feeling may merge within me to become a prayer transcending words.

Another approach would be to follow one theme through the Bible for reflection and response. Certain auxiliary books, such as Albert Gelin's little *Key Concepts of the Old Testament,* can be suggestive and instructive. In a list of such themes Gelin includes, for instance, *faith*: "Faith (man in his relationship to God)—Abraham; Isaiah; Job; Hebrews XI; Romans IV." In connection with Abraham, the author suggests looking into Kierkegaard's *Fear and Trembling.* Pursuing this theme of faith, then, I would begin reading about Abraham (*Genesis* 12 et seq.), reading slowly and thoughtfully, interrupting at striking points or after completed incidents to transform Abraham's experience into my own life, waiting quietly at times for God's enlightening and expanding action in my inner being.

Following Gelin's indication, I would then, in the same manner, peruse Kierkegaard's *Fear and Trembling.* This procedure would be in line with the recommendation of various authors[5] and with my own experience, to alternate in meditating between Scripture and other books.

Pursuing the same method, I would take *Isaiah, Job,* chapter 11 of *Hebrews,* and chapter 4 of *Romans,* as suggested by Gelin. Passages here and there I would skim over if they do not seem to relate to my theme of faith. When I finished a selection, I would concentrate on the whole in its relation to faith.

In between I might like to consult an exegesis of *Isaiah* or *Job* or one of the other passages. Or at least I might clear up some puzzling aspects by referring to a work like McKenzie's *Dictionary of the Bible*. The better I understand the selection on which I am reflecting, the richer will be the flow of my prayer.

A plan such as this would cover weeks of meditation and prayer.

I have been asked how I transform the narrative of the Bible into personal prayer. Each person would have a unique way of making the transition. Mine would be somewhat like the following. Suppose I am reflecting upon the account of Abraham. *Genesis* 12 begins with: "Now the Lord said to Abraham, 'Go from your country and your kindred and your father's house to the land that I will show you." I would probably read to about verse 10.

I would then try to comprehend what it meant to Abraham, in his times and at his age and in his culture of close family ties, to leave his country and his kindred and his father's house, the hardships and heartaches involved. I would try to fathom the nebulosity of the promises, the dangers ahead, his feeling of responsibility for Sarai and Lot and the others he had with him. Twice in the first nine verses, he built an altar to the Lord. God said to him: "To your descendants I will give this land." With the Canaanites occupying the area, this promise seemed hard to believe. But Abraham had faith in his God; and the first altar appears to have been built to express acceptance and thanksgiving. The second altar, built still in an unwavering spirit of faith, may indicate his feeling of need for guidance, for, we are told, "he called on the name of the Lord." And then, although he had already pitched his tent in a defined spot, he "journeyed on."

What is God saying to *me* in this narrative? I am Abraham. God has called me, not once but several times in my life, to make radical moves from places familiar and precious to me, in which I have rooted myself, from persons close and

36

dearly loved, from styles of living and thinking and doing I have cherished and taken for granted, to go to a land he would show me . . . a strange land, a land of risk and challenge. There have been the fearful transition from childhood to adulthood, the call to religious conversion, the choices of careers, the bids to assume responsibilities and formidable tasks, the pull to new and uprooting awarenesses and modes of thinking. I ponder over all of these and relive them. I build an altar in the depths of my being to thank my God and to call on his name to deepen my faith, to lead me on to the fulness of all I was created to be. Here I might remember John Henry Newman's poem, "Lead, Kindly Light" and ponder it and Newman's life as being more like my own life than Abraham's.

Lead, kindly Light, amid the encircling gloom,
Lead thou me on;
The night is dark, and I am far from home,
Lead thou me on.
Keep thou my feet; I do not ask to see
The distant scene; one step enough for me.
I was not ever thus, nor prayed that thou
Shouldst lead me on;
I loved to choose and see my path; but now
Lead thou me on.
I loved the garish day, and spite of fears,
Pride ruled my will: remember not past years. . . .[6]

When I continue my meditation on Abraham, I might read as far as chapter 14. Here Abraham runs into famine; he shows weakness in endangering, for his own self-interest, his relationship with his wife, Sarai. God intervenes to save Sarai and puts Abraham again on the path which will lead to the fulfillment of God's promises to him. When he returns to the spot where he had previously erected an altar to God, he again calls upon the name of the Lord. Problems arise with his nephew Lot, which result in his remaining in the land God

37

had promised him. God again speaks to him, renewing his promise. And Abraham finally settles in that land, building there an altar to the Lord.

Identifying with Abraham, I review periods of famine in my own life—famine in the sense of physical want, and famines intellectual, emotional, and spiritual. I recall temptations; I regret my failures to measure up to what God could have expected of me; and I rediscover God's interventions to save me from the results of my ignorance and weakness and to set me again on a path of progress and fulfillment. Sometimes, in answer to my prayers, vexatious obstacles appeared that indirectly diverted me to the direction later recognized as the best. My understanding of the way of the Lord with me is deepened. My faith in him is strengthened. And I build with love in the depth of my soul "an altar to the Lord." Reading, reflection, and identification form the structure of this mode of prayer.

Certain passages or phrases of Scripture have greater depth and appeal than others, and I dwell on these longer and mark them for repeated probing. In the protracted meditation on faith, suggested by Gelin, for instance, I come upon verses in *Isaiah* to which I go back again and again. One of many other such discoveries is a fragment in *Romans,* chapter 4, which reads: ". . . in the presence of the God in whom he believed, who gives life to the dead and calls into existence the things that do not exist." These lines open up for me days of reflection and response in prayer. I plumb the significance of words and phrases: *presence; God; presence of God; believed; in whom; life; dead; gives; gives life to the dead; calls; existence; calls into existence the things that do not exist.*

Presence. When am I *present* to another? When I am not merely hearing but listening; when I am not just seeing but feeling with; when I am conscious of the other as *other,* unique, yet linked with me by relational bonds. . . . When is another person present to me? . . . What is the situation when that other is God?

38

God. Who is God in relation to me? Conceiver of the idea of me; creator; father and mother; preserver; sustainer; brother and sister; teacher; friend; savior; enlightener; counselor; guide. The Way, the Truth, and the Life. The Living Water. The Bread of Life. The Spirit who abides in me.

The presence of God. The poets often help me in this kind of meditation. Some lines of Gerard Manley Hopkins come to mind to quicken the awareness of the presence of God all around me;

The world is charged with the grandeur of God
It will flame out, like shining from shook foil.

and

. . . the Holy Ghost over the bent
World broods with warm breast and with ah! bright wings.[7]

Can I let myself *go,* to experience the presence of God?

Dead. Dead connotes something that was once alive. I recall that the mouthpieces of the death-conscious twentieth century—contemporary poets, novelists, and dramatists—frequently explore the various concepts of what *dead* means. "And the dead tree gives no shelter," moans T. S. Eliot in *The Waste Land.* What trees that have sheltered *me* are dead and wait for new life? Family life, friendships, nation, church, intellectual growth, ideals, faith, love? Am *I* one of these dead trees, or am I like the tree portrayed in Psalm 1, "a tree planted by streams of water, that yields its fruit in its season, and its leaf does not wither." "God's glory is man fully alive," declares Irenaeus.

I may meditate further on Eliot's poems, those describing the most dreadful of the dead: the half-dead, the living dead.

Under the brown fog of a winter dawn,
A crowd flowed over London Bridge, so many
I had not thought death had undone so many. . . .[8]

39

I think we are in rats' alley
Where the dead men lost their bones . . .[9]

Are you alive or not? Is there nothing in your head?[10]

I have measured out my life with coffee spoons. . . .[11]

Thou hast nor youth nor age
But as it were an after dinner sleep
Dreaming of both. . . .[12]

Can these images help me discern the meaning of this word *dead* in my life and in my world? Can I pray for resurrection, perhaps in the words of Hopkins, "O thou Lord of life, send my roots rain"?[13] Or in the lines of Auden:

Harrow the house of the dead; look shining at
New styles of architecture, a change of heart.[14]

Or, can I look simply to Life, with unspeakable longing.
Gives. What does *gives, gift,* mean? Who is giving, in this quotation from Romans iv?
Gives . . . life . . . to the dead—the dead, my dead that call for new life.
This has happened and is happening. He *called . . .* into the void . . . and I came into existence. I and all the rest of creation were things that did not exist . . . And now, even now, there are *the things that do not exist.* And he is calling them into existence . . . in me . . . in my life . . . in my world . . . in the cosmos . . . in any other possible cosmos. A mystery of anticipation and hope.
In this manner, through exploring the nuances of the words of Scripture, and by assimilating the insights of the poets and seers in the same areas of thought, prayer can be evoked and exercised.
A third function of the Bible in our prayer life is its copious supply of prayers and hymns, so aptly and naturally

articulated that we can adapt them, with ease and a deep feeling of rightness, to our times and the special circumstances of our lives. They seem to flow from the very wellsprings of human nature, so that fundamentally they are never out of date, always satisfying in expressing our profound needs and aspirations.

For almost three thousand years the psalms, for instance, have served as a fountainhead of praise, thanksgiving, repentance, resolution, and petition in public liturgies and personal prayer. They form the most characteristic elements of the Divine Office, the official prayer of the Catholic Church, for example, as well as continuing to be a significant part of Jewish prayer. In Christian rituals they are predominant in the eucharistic and sacramental formulas.

In the course of history some of the psalms have possibly been adapted to the changed circumstances of the times. Modern translations certainly make them more meaningful and moving for contemporary prayer. Because of differences in culture, mention of customs long abandoned, expressions of violence and cruelty, and sometimes the portrayal of an anthropomorphic God strange and foreign to contemporary sensibilities, a few of the psalms do not serve well as prayerful media in our day. Complete psalters have recently appeared adapting the language and imagery of the psalms to a modern stance. One of these is *Psalms Now* by Leslie Brandt.[15] These paraphrases may be the stimulus for significant prayer and a model for personal adaptations. Although many of the older translations are majestic and inspiring, and even more so some of the modern literal versions, still the more drastic updating of the paraphrases ring truer to many modern men and women trying to incorporate the psalms into their prayer. Tastes differ. Each one can choose the style tending most to promote loving prayer.

In addition to the psalms, there are many canticles to be found in various parts of the Bible. These may fit special moods, or may be used as springboards when prayer becomes difficult. In the Old Testament, there are canticles by Moses,

41

Anna, Sirach, Isaiah, Hezekiah, Jeremiah, the three Young Men as recorded in the additions to the book of Daniel, Habakkuk, Tobit, Judith, and others. They express thanksgiving, awe at the splendor and power of God, distress and sorrow, mourning turned into joy, joy in God's creation and in His mercy and goodness to Israel.[16] Of jubilant beauty is the Canticle of the Three Young Men in verses such as these:

Bless the Lord, all works of the Lord,
> sing praise to him and highly exalt him forever.

. . . .

Bless the Lord, sun and moon,
> sing praise to him and highly exalt him forever.
Bless the Lord, stars of heaven,
> sing praise to him and highly exalt him forever.
Bless the Lord, all rain and dew,
> sing praise to him and highly exalt him forever.
Bless the Lord, all winds,
> sing praise to him and highly exalt him forever.
Bless the Lord, fire and heat,
> sing praise to him and highly exalt him forever.
Bless the Lord, winter cold and summer heat,
> sing praise to him and highly exalt him forever.
Bless the Lord, dews and snows,
> sing praise to him and highly exalt him forever.
Bless the Lord, nights and days,
> sing praise to him and highly exalt him forever.
Bless the Lord, light and darkness,
> sing praise to him and highly exalt him forever.
Bless the Lord ice and cold,
> sing praise to him and highly exalt him forever.
Bless the Lord, frosts and snows,
> sing praise to him and highly exalt him forever.
Bless the Lord, lightnings and clouds,
> sing praise to him and highly exalt him forever.
Let the earth bless the Lord:

let it sing praise to him and highly exalt him forever.
Bless the Lord, mountains and hills,
   sing praise to him and highly exalt him forever.
Bless the Lord, all things that grow on the earth,
   sing praise to him and highly exalt him forever.
Bless the Lord, you springs,
   sing praise to him and highly exalt him forever.
Bless the Lord, seas and rivers,
   sing praise to him and highly exalt him forever.
Bless the Lord, you whales and all creatures that move
     in the waters,
   sing praise to him and highly exalt him forever.
Bless the Lord, all birds of the air,
   sing praise to him and highly exalt him forever.
Bless the Lord, all beasts and cattle,
   sing praise to him and highly exalt him forever.
Bless the Lord, you sons of men,
   sing praise to him and highly exalt him forever.

.   .   .   .

Give thanks to the Lord, for he is good,
   for his mercy endures forever.

    The canticle of Hezekiah, appearing in the book of
Isaiah, poignantly expresses affliction and grief:

.   .   .   .

My dwelling is plucked up and removed from me
   like a shepherd's tent;
like a weaver I have rolled up my life;
   he cuts me off from the loom;

.   .   .   .

like a lion he breaks all my bones;
   from day to night thou dost bring me to an end.

.   .   .   .

But what can I say? For he has spoken to me,
   and he himself has done it.

All my sleep has fled
    because of the bitterness of my soul.
O Lord, by these things men live,
    and in all these is the life of my spirit.
    Oh, restore me to health and make me live.
Lo, it was for my welfare
    that I had great bitterness;
but thou hast held back my life
    from the pit of destruction,
for thou hast cast all my sins
    behind thy back.

.   .   .   .

The living, the living he thanks thee
    as I do this day;
the father makes known to the children
    thy faithfulness; . . .

Besides these shorter lyrical passages, we have the *Canticle of Canticles,* or *Song of Songs* as it is more widely known, which constitutes a canonical book of the Old Testament. Among its various disputed interpretations is that of mystics who see in it an expression of love between God and the individual soul. Its figures and images express a daring love that should not be denied the most authentic of love relationships, that between God and the loved one he has created for himself.

My beloved speaks and says to me
"Arise, my love, my fair one,
    and come away;
for lo, the winter is past,
    the rain is over and gone.
The flowers appear on the earth,
    the time of singing has come,
and the voice of the turtledove
    is heard in our land.
The fig tree puts forth its figs,

and the vines are in blossom;
they give forth fragrance.
Arise, my love, my fair one, and come away."
.   .   .   .

Upon my bed by night
I sought him whom my soul loves;
I sought him but found him not;
    I called him, but he gave no answer.
"I will rise now and go about the city,
    in the streets and in the squares;
I will seek him whom my soul loves."
    I sought him, but found him not.
The watchmen found me,
    as they went about in the city.
"Have you seen him whom my soul loves?"
Scarcely had I passed them,
    when I found him whom my soul loves.
I held him, and would not let him go
    until I had brought him into my mother's house,
    and into the chamber of her that conceived me. . . .

St. John of the Cross's poem "The Spiritual Canticle"
echoes much of the *Song of Songs* in its delineation of mystical progress as he divined it.

Where have you hidden away?
Never a crumb of comfort day or night,
    Dearest? To wound your prey
    and off like a stag in flight!
I hurried forth imploring you—out of sight!

You shepherds, you that rove
up in the ranches on the mountain's brow,
    if you should meet my love,
    my one love, tell him how
I'm heartsick, fevered, and fast sinking now.
.   .   .   .

45

O groves and leafy screen,
foliage planted by a lover's hand,
    meadows of bluegreen
    with marigolds japanned,
tell me, has he been lately in your land?[17]

Three canticles of the New Testament assume importance in the official morning, evening, and night prayer of
the Catholic Church. The *Benedictus*,[18] canticle of Zechariah,
father of John the Baptist, is a permanent part of Lauds, the
authorized early morning prayer. A chant of thanksgiving
and hope, it proposes a program of life to the person who
identifies with it. Beginning with "Blessed be the Lord God of
Israel, for he has visited and redeemed his people," it later
addresses the individual:

And you, child, will be called
    the prophet of the Most High;
for you will go before the Lord
    to prepare his ways,
to give knowledge of salvation
    to his people
    in the forgiveness of their sins,
through the tender mercy of our God,
when the days shall dawn upon us from on high
to give light to those who sit in darkness
    and in the shadow of death,
to guide our feet into the way of peace.

What an assignment is this, given to each of us, at the
dawn of every day!
The Canticle of Mary, the *Magnificat*,[19] forms part of
Vespers, the late afternoon or evening prayer. It, too, is a
song of thanksgiving and praise.

My soul magnifies the Lord,
and my spirit rejoices in God my Savior.

.   .   .   .

for he who is mighty has done great things for me,
and holy is his name.

.   .   .   .

he has filled the hungry with good things,
and the rich he has sent empty away.

Adapted by Mary from the ancient canticle of Anna,[20] it reveals how deeply the mother of Jesus was steeped in the sacred writings of her people and how adept she was in assuming them personally as her own. Since this process is just what we have been trying to follow, the *Magnificat* may be a model for us. A personal attempt to adjust it to contemporary language and imagery would be a most meaningful and soul-moving exercise in prayer.

The Canticle of Simeon,[21] called the *Nunc Dimittis* from the first two Latin words, is an appropriate part of night prayer. Simeon, an aged man of God, had just seen Jesus carried as a baby in the arms of his mother into the Temple in Jerusalem. He prays:

Now, Lord, you may dismiss your servant
    in peace, according to your word:
For my eyes have seen your salvation,
    which you have set before all the nations,
As a light of revelation for the Gentiles
    and the glory of your people Israel.

Our night's sleep is an image of death, the death of each day. Since early morning we have been witnessing and experiencing the supportive action of God in our lives and in our world. He has been revealing himself in nature, in people, in development, and hopefully we have grown in understanding him and his way with us, and in trusting his design

47

for us and his care. In this trust, then, we go in peace to our sleep—or, as it will one time be, to our death.

Besides the psalms and canticles, the "Our Father" provides one of the most profound prayer experiences in making it our own. One way to accomplish this, is to explore each word and phrase for its hidden meanings and for the personal applications to ourselves. *Father*. What does this word mean to me? What do I think Jesus intended it to mean? Incorporated in Jesus as I am, what does it means to me through him? *Our*. Why *our* and not *my?* In what relation to others does this place me, right at the beginning of my prayer? *Heaven*. Does this necessarily mean "up there"? Can it mean "perfect happiness" or "communion"? Can the word connote the majesty, power, glory, the transcendence of God? Can it be a term of reference to the presence of God, found as he is at the core of all entities? . . . And on through the prayer to the word *evil*. What is the evil from which I am asking God to deliver me? What are the real evils in my world? What must I be doing about these myself?

Another moving gospel prayer is that of Jesus at the Last Supper, as recorded by John in chapter 17. We must go to Jesus to learn how to pray; and here is one of the rare instances when we have his prayer expressed in words. We notice again the intimacy of the address, "Father." We wonder at his petitions for his apostles: "keep them . . . that they may be one, even as we are one; . . . that they may have my joy fulfilled in themselves. . . . Sanctify them in the truth . . ." We are moved, for these requests are not for the apostles only, but also for us, as he prays: "I do not pray for these only, but also for those who believe in me through their words, that they may all be one; even as thou, Father art in me, and I in thee, that they also may be in us, so that the world may believe that thou hast sent me. . . . Father, I desire that they also, whom thou hast given me, may be with me where I am. . . ."

Scattered through the Gospels also are many short prayers that fit easily to our hearts and lips on appropriate

48

occasions. The song of the angels in Luke 2: "Glory to God in the highest, and on earth peace among men . . ." The prayer of the father of the boy with the dumb spirit: "if you can do anything, have pity on us and help us." And Jesus said to him, "If you can! All things are possible to him who believes." Immediately the father of the child cried out, "I believe; help my unbelief!"[22] The blind beggar Bartimaeus pleaded: "Master, let me receive my sight."[23] Life is difficult for us because we are blind in many areas. The centurion asked for the cure of his servant: "Lord, I am not worthy to have you come under my roof; but only say the word, and my servant will be healed."[24] *Servant* can be the symbol for any need we have.

Throughout the epistles are blessings, especially as greetings and farewells in the letters, and exclamations of praise and thanksgiving. At the end of Romans 11 occurs a sublime acclamation:

O the depth of the riches and wisdom and knowledge
    of God!
How unsearchable are his judgments and how
    inscrutable His ways!
"For who has known the mind of the Lord,
or who has been his counselor?"
"Or who has given a gift to him
that he might be repaid?"
For from him and through him and to him are all
    things.
To him be glory forever. Amen.

Ephesians 3 also ends with a comprehensive prayer that might well be adapted for any person or group:

For this reason I bow my knees before the Father, from whom every family in heaven and on earth is named, that according to the riches of his glory he may grant you to be strengthened with might through his Spirit in

49

the inner man, and that Christ may dwell in your hearts through faith; that you, being rooted and grounded in love, may have power to comprehend with all the saints what is the breadth and length and height and depth, and to know the love of Christ which surpasses knowledge, that you may be filled with all the fulness of God.

Second Thessalonians 2 closes with a little jewel of prayer:

Now may our Lord Jesus Christ himself, and God our Father, who loved us and gave us eternal comfort and good hope through grace, comfort your hearts and establish them in every good work and word.

The examples proffered in this chapter are only meager samplings of the riches the sacred writings offer for our prayer. They may provide some different approaches to expanding prayer through a deepening knowledge of God's revelation of himself, through various uses of biblical passages for reflective meditation and response, and through a heightened awareness of the treasure of inspired prayer hidden in Holy Scripture.

CHAPTER 7

Liturgical Prayer

Liturgical prayer and mystical prayer are expressions of two different facets of human nature. Mystical prayer has to do with the unique, individual, personal quest for God, and liturgical prayer with the social and public aspects. In a way, mystical prayer is an inner, quiet aloneness with God, while liturgical prayer is an outward celebration of him. Of course, mystical prayer must infuse liturgical prayer to keep it from lapsing into "sounding brass and tinkling cymbals." And liturgical prayer must draw out the contemplative into the social areas of human wholeness. Both are necessary for spiritual journeying.

To focus upon liturgical prayer at this time seems urgent, because it is presently in a state of confusion and flux. The importance of liturgy to our spiritual growth emerges from the fact that it is the ritual prayer of the community and we are by our human nature social and symbol/ritual-making creatures. Perhaps we need to review the evidence for this last assertion. It may help our understanding of the situation to examine also why we are at this point where we are liturgically, and what are some of the feasible developments for the present and future.

First, then, why is the liturgy of importance to us? Dur-

51

ing recent decades, depth psychologists and anthropologists have uncovered much concerning what we may call the basic or primary needs of human beings. This research is continuing to reveal invaluable new aspects of both the negative and positive dimensions of human development.

Carl Jung, for example, has given us new insights into ourselves through his exploration of the collective unconscious and its archetypes. He defines archetypes as archaic psychic remnants "which seem to be aboriginal, innate, and inherited shapes of the human mind."[1] They resemble the remnants of biological evolution found in nature as a whole and in our own bodies, especially in the passage of the foetus through the various evolutionary stages. Among the psychic "instincts" are religious, social, and symbol-producing archetypes.

In our consideration of prayer, these innate psychic drives must be kept in mind. Much of our present public prayer developed during the Middle Ages and Renaissance and became institutionalized. The fact that much of it is no longer meaningful to us in the age of science and technology does not indicate that we can with impunity dispense with all liturgy and the ritual through which it expresses itself. The dynamic archetypes in our unconscious, which move us to express symbolically as a social group our religious propensities, if ignored or repressed, will create disturbances both within individuals in their drive to become whole human beings, and within society. Such ignoring could well be contributing to what is happening in many persons throughout the world today, resulting in alienation, violence, lack of purpose, ennui.

Relevant to the need to express our religious tendencies as a group, sciences dealing with primitive man give evidence that the emergence of the individual from the tribe was a relatively recent evolutionary step. As late as the Jewish Scriptures, the writers refer to the Hebrew people in the singular, as Israel. Among primitive peoples still in existence, we can verify this trend, where individual members cannot conceive of themselves as separate from the tribe. Even among

52

modern men and women who value and consciously work at individuation, our social roots are not questioned. We need a father and a mother for conception. We need a family to care for us over a long period of time. We need the community to educate us, to pass on to us the accumulated heritage of knowledge, skills, and spiritual values. We need laws and government to secure order and justice. We need economic interchange to survive. And because we are more than animals and have characteristically human needs to be satisfied, we especially need a common culture in which to root ourselves.

In like manner, we need the security and support of our society's recognition of God. Prehistoric evidences of public worship have been discovered in widely separated spots on our earth. Associated with these are certain common symbols that have led Jung and others to posit in the human psyche innate tendencies to symbolization along definite lines. Aniela Jaffé points out the rock, the circle, and the animal as examples of sacred symbols, appearing from prehistoric times to the present.[2] Around ancient sacred spots myths arose to explain the symbols; and rituals, often acting out the myths, originated. Other myths make us aware of numerous symbols less enduring than rocks and carvings on them or more difficult to represent: wind, water, plants, sun, moon. Besides natural objects, man-made things (dwellings, means of transportation, weapons) and abstract forms (numbers, geometrical figures) assumed symbolic roles. According to Jung, symbols, originating in long-forgotten psychic sources, have from prehistoric times nourished philosophical and religious speculations about life and death.[3]

To our ancestors of prehistoric and early historical periods, the cosmos was sacred. Life emerged from sacral mystery, and the places and the times concerned with life were holy.[4] Human beings expressed this intuition by ritual, a "strange, universal phenomenon."[5] Suzanne Langer, in her scholarly treatise, *Philosophy in a New Key,* calls ritual "the language of religion,"[6] and religion "the most typical and fundamental edifice of the human mind."[7] "I believe," she declares, "there is a primary need in man, which other creatures probably do not have, and which actuates all his apparently unzoological aims, his wistful fancies, his consciousness of value, his utterly impractical enthusiasms, and his awareness of a 'Beyond' filled with holiness."[8]

From myths, from the ruins of antique temples and dwellings, and from the relics of sculptured representations of ancient customs, we are aware then of public worship as far back as men and women have left us any records of themselves. Socially rooted as they were, human beings, before the mists of prehistory cleared, had settled upon symbols and rituals that they recognized and shared as a group in their worship of the holy.[9] Coexistent with human evolution as this tendency seems to be, it would appear reasonable to accept it as innate and necessary. And if this is so, the contemporary withdrawal from symbolism and ritual apparent in our culture is a diminishment of human growth and wholeness. It may be time for us to reanimate this spiritual instinct for community celebration of the sacred, by reviving our understanding of universal religious symbols and by creating relevant new symbols, occasions, and rituals for our liturgical prayer.

Liturgy is the name given to the official form of public worship. From the history of all religions certain elements of liturgy can be deduced, elements more or less richly developed according to place, time, and stage of culture.

Given an awareness of the divine presence, ancient people designated the *place* as holy by setting up a stone, an altar, a shrine, a temple. Perhaps the place itself was seen as sacred —a mountain, a valley, a river, a spring.

A *time* for celebration, commemoration, and petition emerged according to the nature of the divine manifestation, renewed perhaps seasonally (such as at the solstices) or cyclically in smaller or greater cycles (such as at the full moon or at the beginning of the year or at harvest time), or occasionally according to significant circumstances (such as a marriage, a death, a military victory).

54

Appropriate *rites* became customary, embellished by accepted symbolic *gestures*; perhaps processions or dances became traditional; and frequently characteristic *music* became associated with the rite.

The other arts, too—architecture, sculpture, painting, glasswork, poetry, drama, handicraft—flourished more or less according to area, period, and people, in efforts to beautify and make significant the sacred place or occasion. In all this an *archetypal* symbolism is evident throughout the ages and on all parts of the earth.[10]

As societies grew more complex and religions developed, full-time *ministers* for the temples and rituals became necessary. Priests and priestesses, vestal virgins, monks, shamans took on the care of the holy places, organized the liturgies, and received the participating people.

Since Christianity emerged slowly from Judaism, it is understandable that Hebrew traditions and customs remained the base for developing Christian forms of worship. The books of the Hebrew Scripture were still sacred to the early Christians, and the Gospels, Acts, Epistles, and the Book of Revelation were gradually added. The myths, history, symbols, language, and regulations of the ancient Scriptures were carried along as a natural heritage. After all, their whole purport was seen to point to the Messiah, who had now come and fulfilled the types, figures, and prophecies of the books of the Jews. The first Christians continued to attend the synagogues and observe the accustomed Hebrew liturgies and rituals, celebrating the Christian "breaking of the bread" apart in their homes. Baptism was not an unusual custom among the Jews, as is evidenced by the practice of John the Baptist. It simply took on a new significance in Christianity.

Not until the Gentiles began to join the disciples of Jesus did the question arise concerning the relevance of certain Jewish rites in the Christian age. St. Paul had to fight for exemption from circumcision and dietary restrictions for his Gentile neophytes. These rituals, he declared, had prepared for the Christ, who had now come. Gradually Jewish ele-

55

ments in the liturgy were either eliminated or translated into a Christian setting.

In Gentile countries, similarly, the evolution of Christian liturgy often took on the form of purified local rites. The felt need of these early Christians was a liturgical decorum for proclaiming the Good News, for expressing the Christian experience in baptism and the Eucharist, and for carrying out the commandment of love. These three requirements are the basic liturgical criteria for our times as well.

As history moved into the Middle Ages, characteristic modes of architecture, of music, of ceremonies, of ministering to others sprang out of the creative instincts of peoples in keeping with place and time. The synagogue and the Greek and Roman temples and places of assembly had served as early models for basic structure. In the East, Byzantine symbolism and art forms embellished this architectural plan; and in the West, the round Greek and Roman arches and domes gradually thrust upward into the pointed and spired Gothic translations of the movement of the spirit.

Early Christian music, of course, consisted of Hebrew chants. New compositions were expressed in the prevailing Greek modes. Pope Gregory I collected in his *Antiphonale Missarum* many of the chants being used by the time of the sixth century, thus giving an approved model for church music, which became known as Gregorian chant.

In the cathedrals and monasteries, spread over Europe from the fourth century on, highly symbolic rituals developed, sometimes starting with pre-Christian local celebrations. With monks and missionaries who maintained ties with the Roman church fanning out into all parts of the known world, a degree of uniformity subsisted.

Schools, hospices for pilgrims, and varied arrangements for caring for the sick and homeless grew in connection with monasteries and sometimes with the cathedrals. Schools were often song- and liturgy-related. Hospitality and care for the poor overflowed from the liturgy as acts of love of Christ, who said, "What you do for the least of my brethren you do for me."[11]

By the time of the Renaissance, the monasteries were declining. But the drama of the Mass had solidified in structure, the church year was set in form, the monastic hours were an integral part of the liturgy, and the symbolism of the ritual had developed. The Renaissance added splendor, strengthening the trend toward monarchical attitudes and trappings in liturgical ceremonies. Because of the deep interest in the arts, the competitiveness of patrons, and the wide flowering of artistic genius, the embellishment of buildings and articles used for religious purposes reached astounding proportions. To match this magnificence, liturgical events became more and more extravagant. Polyphonic music overshadowed the simple Gregorian chants, and musical instruments became more numerous and sophisticated.

Then came the Protestant revolution, one aspect of which was reaction against these excesses in decoration, in pageantry, in intricate music. Some sects went to the extreme of eliminating all decoration, ritual, and music except for simple hymns in the vernacular. To stem this Protestant revolt in Christendom, the Council of Trent set up regulatory codes that rigidified the teaching and practice of the Catholic Church for centuries. Gradually the fixed liturgy became less and less the religious expression of the times. The language—Latin and Greek—was understood by few. The rural symbolism became increasingly meaningless to the teeming people of the cities. And besides the fact that cultural customs had changed radically, liturgical gestures and vestments had become so formalized that the original reasons for their use grew obscure. Most people attended religious ceremonies as obligations under pain of sin rather than as meaningful opportunities for conveying their religious feelings and insights. "Devotions" like the rosary and novenas became more significant to the masses of the people than the legal liturgical formulas bearing the authentic Christian message.

A reconsideration of the liturgy by the Church was long overdue by the time of the Vatican II Council. *The Constitution on the Sacred Liturgy* was the first of the Council documents to be completed and published. Parts of it rapidly became outdated. It was thought by some to lack depth. For the most part, however, what the document did present has not been absorbed by the greater number of the clergy whose seminary studies preceded Vatican II, or by the majority of the laity, many of whom have not even heard of the document.

The primary emphasis of the Vatican II pronouncement concerning the liturgy is on the active participation of the *people* in the official worship of God. "In the restoration and promotion of the sacred liturgy," the document declares, "this full and active participation by all the people is the aim to be considered before all else."[12]

The need for change is also stressed. "Liturgy," notes the document, "is made up of unchangeable elements divinely instituted, and elements subject to change. The latter not only may but ought to be changed with the passing of time if features have by chance crept in which are less harmonious with the intimate nature of the liturgy, or if existing elements have grown less functional."[13] Changes may involve a return to some earlier, simpler forms, adapted to needs brought about by radical alterations in our environment and society. Or, even more important, changes may occur by the creation of new symbols and rites springing out of a new age. Today, one of the challenges of adult Catholics, both clerical and lay, is to recognize the "unchangeable elements" and to work at understanding them and making them meaningful for our age; and, at the same time, to supplant irrelevant rites with dynamic and life-stirring replacements.

In the document on the liturgy, the Church Council also put emphasis on the training of the clergy in liturgy and on their obligation to instruct the people and to include them wherever possible. The fact that many of the clergy have been slow in implementing the council's updating of the liturgy is no excuse for the lack of involvement of the people as a whole. *The Constitution on the Sacred Liturgy* lays down the basic rules for all to read, and makes very clear the priestly function of the whole people of God. Where the leadership of the clergy exists, cooperation and encouragement on the part of the people is a sacred obligation. Where this leadership does not exist, it is the responsibility of the people of God to inform themselves of the promptings of the Holy Spirit as revealed through the Council in this regard, and to prudently and tactfully promote the implementation of the Constitution.

The Constitution on the Sacred Liturgy makes clear that any consideration of the relevancy of liturgy should be made from historical, theological, and pastoral perspectives. In all these aspects the importance of sacred Scripture is stressed by the document. It seems then that the mature responsibility of the people of God in contemporary times is to deepen their comprehension of history, theology, Scripture, and symbolic expression in order to reconsider, from a modern pastoral point of view, the elements of liturgy and their possible elaboration in relation to our age and needs. We want, of course, to retain what is valuable in our heritage. But we are impelled also to create real expressions of our contemporary approach to God, expressions meaningful to our times.

With further regard to *history,* many present-day Catholics have rejected most of the plan of Christian growth bequeathed to us by our ancestors. Or perhaps they were not even aware of it as a plan, so encumbered had it become with outmoded symbolism that had never been explained adequately or made a real part of life. It might be well to reflect on this plan to determine how much of it, if understood, could be applicable today.

There exists, for instance, the great overall program for life, the sacramental system, beginning with baptism at the outset of life, touching on significant phases of life in the reception of the Eucharist, reconciliation, confirmation, matri-

59

mony and holy orders, and ending with the sacrament of the sick and dying. This series of holy events is a life-infusing design for the whole of our earthly existence and mission, if understood and accepted. By its very definition *sacra-ment* means contact with the sacred. At significant points in our growth as Christians, God literally touches us. His touch is grace-giving, making it possible for us to transcend our natural human limits. The sacrament is an outward sign, signifying by symbolic ritual the nature of the divine action taking place.

Then there is the liturgical year, an annual schema for Christian maturing. Uniting us with Christ as the Way, the Truth, and the Life,[14] it aims to lead us through the entire Christ-experience each year, hopefully each time at a higher level of growth. Beginning with a period of preparation, Advent, we experience liturgically a new beginning in the Christmas season, advance through a reexamination of Christ's teaching and deeds, enter with him in Lent into his suffering and death for our salvation, and rise again with him at Easter into the mystery of life after death. At Pentecost we are filled again with the Holy Spirit and are reinvested with our responsibilities to carry on Christ's mission in our world. The rest of the year focuses upon the ways to accomplish the task we are privileged to share.

Among the inherited liturgical offerings, there is even a prayer plan for each day—the Divine Office, the official prayer of the Church. Since its post-Vatican II revision, it is more commonly called the Liturgy of the Hours. *The Constitution on Sacred Liturgy* devotes a chapter to this valued custom. Following the Liturgical Year, the Liturgy of the Hours sanctifies each part of the day, presenting in the spirit of the liturgical season relevant psalms for the time of day being celebrated. Passages from Scripture, selections from the writings of the early Fathers of the Church, the popes, and modern authors, biographies of the saints, and explanations of certain solemn celebrations, provide daily instruction. While ordained clergy and certain religious orders are bound to the prayer of the Divine Office, all the people of God are encouraged to participate in it as far as circumstances permit, either together with those obligated to it, in groups among themselves, or individually.[15] When they do this, they are uniting with Christ and with the people of God the whole world over in continual prayer to God. There is a sense of unity and solidarity in sharing the official prayer of Christ's Church as it blends from all part of the globe, offering praise, thanksgiving, repentance, and petition in the name of all the people of God.

Having moved from the liturgical *life* scope of the sacraments, to the liturgical *year,* to the sanctification of the *day* through the Divine Office, we focus finally on the one act which is central to Christian liturgy, the celebration of the eucharist. The chapter of *The Constitution on the Sacred Liturgy* entitled "The Most Sacred Mystery of the Eucharist" begins with this paragraph:

> At the Last Supper, on the night when He was betrayed, our Savior instituted the Eucharistic Sacrifice of His Body and Blood. He did this in order to perpetuate the sacrifice of the Cross throughout the centuries until He should come again, and so to entrust to . . . the Church a memorial of His death and resurrection: a sacrament of love, a sign of unity, a bond of charity, a paschal banquet in which Christ is consumed, the mind is filled with grace, and a pledge of future glory is given to us.[16]

The document goes on to outline the revision of the ritual forms surrounding the essential elements of the Mass to attune this mystery of faith more with contemporary understanding. This revision will be an ongoing process until the apathy and alienation that now pretty generally prevail give way to a realization of and enthusiasm for this eloquent contact with God. Many seem to have lost awareness of what the Mass is. A thoughtful meditation on the paragraph just quoted from the *Constitution on the Sacred Liturgy* will surely convince us that here are roots from which a full Christian life may grow.

Retrieved then from history and plumbed to its depth for its riches, our liturgical heritage will offer elements we moderns may wish to intensify, adapt, or build upon.

Theology, another background study in the formation of a meaningful liturgy, is the touchstone for authenticity. Liturgy is an expression of the theology held by those who participate in its rites. Like any other science, theology is constantly expanding its insights, and continual updating is required both by its experts and by all the people of God. Moreover, our powers of perception mature with age, knowledge, and experience. Unfortunately, some seem to operate all their lives on a childish or adolescent theology. So sublime is the subject matter of theology that no human being can ever master it but must continue searching and finding as long as life lasts. Not being experts ourselves, we must turn to the scholars for information, making ourselves aware of theological trends and keeping ourselves open to the new insights of the masters in the field.

As the *Constitution on the Sacred Liturgy* further declares, it is from *Scripture* "that actions and signs derive their meaning." The readings and interludes for the liturgy have traditionally been from this source, and homilies, prayers, and songs have been scriptural in their inspiration. For these reasons, says the document, "if the restoration, progress, and adaptation of the sacred liturgy are to be achieved, it is necessary to promote . . . warm and living love for Scripture."[17] Scripture, too, is a study we must keep ongoing.

A full Christian life involves the whole person, that individual person's maturing of all human areas of potential: physical, intellectual, feeling, social, aesthetic, religious. Accordingly, our liturgical life must stimulate all these areas: our physical selves must participate, our intellects must be challenged, our emotions aroused, our social responsibilities exercised, our need for beauty satisfied, and our innate quest for God led on. Our selections from Holy Scripture and our symbols and rituals must be comprehensive and varied enough to touch all these facets of our being.

As they have evolved, the rites of the sacramental system, the Liturgical Year, the Divine Office, and the Eucharistic celebration are expressed to us in a wealth of symbolism, which, if we are to appreciate the liturgy fully, we must make deeply our own or replace with symbols and rituals which we can make deeply our own.

To accomplish this, a thoughtful, specific study of symbols is important. Symbols have been defined as "material things, things we taste or see or touch, used to signify some reality lying on a deeper or higher level than the purely material. They signify realities either too big to think about comfortably, or too mysterious for the mind to grapple with directly."[18] They are signs to indicate a reality or experience for which words are inadequate.

We have already considered the supposition that we are innately symbol-producing creatures. As an example, let us contemplate one symbol found in our most ancient literature and still significant, that of *journey*: the journey of life, the quest for God. Models from antiquity are Homer's *Odyssey* and the Book of Exodus. The symbol occurs in practically all the racial mythologies and is the framework for most of the great epics. We see it in various aspects of our liturgy: in the range of the sacraments from birth to death; in the progression of the Liturgical Year through the reliving of Christ's journey of life in our own growth; in the advancement of the day in the Liturgy of the Hours; and in Christ's and our own journey through suffering, death, and resurrection reenacted in the Mass. A physical representation of the journey symbol is the *procession*. At a funeral, for instance, the entrance procession is symbolic of the whole of life's pilgrimage as preparation for entering our eternal home in God.

Other timeless symbols are the ancient natural elements of earth, air, water, and fire, which provide a plenitude of signs to express more effectively than words mysteries being encountered. Separated from these elements in their natural

63

form by the pavements, walls, glass, and technology of our cities, human beings seem to suffer an alienation from creation as a whole. There is evident a restlessness, particularly in our city-bred population, to touch base with the components of nature. How satisfying and relaxing are our contacts with nature in its varied constituents: ocean, lake, river, rain; sand, rock, loam, and the plant beauty that springs out of them; clean air for breathing, breezes, winds for sailing and flying; sun, campfires, and open fireplaces! We journey distances to blend our spirits with the spirit of nature emanating from its manifold aspects, and experience a healing though evanescent wholeness. These elements of nature arouse within us deep emotions, which carry over to their use as symbols.

If we allow ourselves to meditate on these natural elements and to experience their innerness, we can transform their material and factual existence to symbols of the spiritual realities we crave. Poets and painters and prophets and prayers have, from times before history, made this transcendent leap. Individually each of us has experienced it in quiet moments with nature. *Earth* in one form or another has *meant* more than its chemical constituents; it has meant home, security, solidity, journeys, the source of life and fruitfulness, repose in death. *Water* has stood for refreshment, cleanliness —of soul as well as of body, of depth and mystery, of danger and adventure, and again, of life and growth, and of journey. *Air* has signified for us spirit, freedom, energy. And *fire* has symbolized love, power, insight, comfort. All of these elements manifest positive and negative, constructive and destructive qualities and signs. Used as symbols, they have the power to arouse our feelings, exercise our intellects, and stimulate our imaginations.

The ceremonies of baptism illustrate the multileveled appeal of symbols. *Water,* of course, is the principal symbol. But there are also *fire* (candle), *earth* (salt and oil), and *air* (breathing of the minister on the one being baptized). Each of these expresses for baptism all the connotative meanings just listed and more. Then there are the other symbols: the white robe, indicative of freedom from sin, and the godparents, representing the Christian community receiving the child as one of its own.

Among the questions, then, for which Christians today need to find the answers with regard to liturgy seem to be: What symbols are no longer meaningful to us and with what significant symbols can we replace them? This includes language; words are also symbols. What are we trying to express by our symbols? How can we deepen our own and others' understanding of the symbols we use?[19] And how can liturgy impel us toward more loving community and more responsible service in the world?

The study of history, theology, sacred scripture, and symbolism can provide answers for the first three of these questions. But the fourth query—how can liturgy impel us toward more loving community and more responsible service in the world?—raises a problem of a different sort. In spite of the great hope placed on the reform of the liturgy during and after the Vatican II Council, the sad truth faces us that the changes introduced have not brought about the renewal prophesied by the document on sacred liturgy: that the faithful would become "of one heart in love," and that the faithful would be drawn into the compelling love of Christ that would set them on fire.[20] People are not being drawn, it seems, into a unity in love, and people are not being inspired to move beyond the church to become Christs in this needful world.

Two weaknesses of the document on liturgy contribute to this failure. Its language is antiquated and churchy, hard to understand. And more importantly, the document distorts the image of Christian life by placing the liturgy in the center of it. Christ did not set the liturgy up as a test by which we would be known as his disciples. He came to save the world; and if we are to be extensions of him, that is what we must be about. God does not need our liturgies; *we* need them for our support, our refreshment, our healing. But they are not the center of our life. We find God in the liturgy, to be sure, but we find him even more in every aspect of his world that

65

needs our care. The prophet Isaiah cries out with words we can still meditate on with benefit:

> Bring no more vain offerings;
> incense is an abomination to me.
> New moon and sabbath and the
> calling of assemblies—
> *I cannot endure iniquity and*
> *solemn assembly.*
> Your new moons and your appointed feasts
> my soul hates;
> they have become a burden to me,
> I am weary of bearing them.
> When you spread forth your hands,
> I will hide my eyes from you;
> even though you make many prayers,
> I will not listen;
> your hands are full of blood.
> Wash yourselves; make yourselves clean;
> remove the evil of your doings
> from before my eyes;
> cease to do evil;
> learn to do good;
> seek justice,
> correct oppression;
> defend the fatherless,
> plead for the widow.[21]

God is clearly saying through the prophet that our liturgies disgust him if we are not seeking justice, correcting oppression. Our liturgies must center around casting out the injustice and oppression of our world: racism, poverty, inequality, greed, violence. Perhaps, as some authors suggest, the true center is there, in Christian community, reaching out of these acts of Christ's love.[22]

What I am trying to say is that those of us who are seeking a more meaningful and supporting liturgy have to look for ways by which liturgies overflow into Christian acts of community and ministry; or, conversely, that liturgies originate in such acts.

It is significant that a recent liturgical week, sponsored annually by the Liturgical Conference of the United States, focused on "The Church as a Ministering Community." One of the goals was "to design and share a vision of the church as a community in which our deepest needs are met and the gifts of all are engaged in service, *diakonia*." The thesis of the Conference was that "service, diakonia, *is* Christian life, that until our love is 'exercised' we are not quite alive, not quite persons—and since diakonia *is* Christian life, it is imperative that the *whole* community be engaged in ministry in one way or another."[23]

Of course, we must occasionally *celebrate* our Christian life, too. Jesus came to bring us the Good News. As one author declares, "I can be told that today is my birthday, and life is a gift, and people love me, but I still want a party, not a fact sheet." And so there are times of unmixed rejoicing in liturgical festivities: the births of various kinds, the milestones, the victories, the resurrections.

In preparing the liturgy there are still some other questions to ask. What is to be the focus of this celebration? Is there a world, national, or parish situation or event around which we should be uniting as Christians? If so, what are the symbols and rituals we can use to express our Christian unity and concern? Should we carry to the altar food, clothing, medicine as symbols of what we are doing or plan to do for those recent disaster victims? Can we communicate how to help the prisoner go free (many kinds of prisoners), the blind receive their sight (many kinds of blind), and any other of the least of his and our brothers and sisters be relieved in their need? Should we have interpretive dancers to ritualize our emotions concerning stirring events? Should we light candles, release balloons, dramatize the cause of our joy or sorrow? Can we tie up with the feast or the gospel of the day significant situations within our community: the plight of the elderly, the handicapped, the immigrants, the unemployed, the lonely, the alienated? What would be the symbols of our concern? How could we translate our symbols into actual service?

There are some other penetrating questions, too. What does it mean for the Spirit to come to our parish or to this special occasion? How can we show that the cup of communion is shared life, the cup of joy and sorrow? Where has the resurrection *just happened,* and what kind of death is threatening now?

If we can make the Scripture and the symbolism of our liturgies come alive in our Christian community and ministry, or if we can express through liturgy what community means and what extending Christ's love to his world means, we shall be able as better integrated and more whole persons to unite with one another in the full celebration of meaningful liturgical prayer.

Epilogue

Spiritual journeys must be personal. We are all questing for God, consciously or unconsciously; but the unique persons that we are and the varied circumstances of all our paths will make each of our journeys different and special.

The directions offered in this little book are sound and trustworthy. God is there in nature, in others, in the depths of my own being; and his voice will always be indicating the way to me if I learn to hear him and to recognize his signs.

Through mystical prayer, I can communicate with him in all times and through all contingencies. Scriptural prayer will be an unfailing source of new insights concerning all aspects of my spiritual quest. And right liturgical prayer can provide the supportive bond with others I require by my very human nature for furthering my search for the Source of my being. Through the word of the liturgy and the human and divine sharing, I cannot fail to grow in knowledge and grace along the way.

There is not the high road of prayer and the low road of daily living in my world. The two must be fused into one road if I am to reach my destination.

God does it all and I do it all in a mysterious teamwork. I am never alone on my spiritual journeying.

APPENDIX

A Sketch of the History of Mysticism

Archaeologists and paleontologists have drawn our attention to hints of man's early mystical tendencies: the discovery, for instance, that man was burying his dead in the early Stone Ages; that gifts were left in the graves; that cave paintings may have been intended as dynamistic, that is, means of animistic control of the animals man hunted. These indications seem to indicate that primitive man was reaching to plumb the transcendent and had formulated some conclusions regarding it.

Anthropologists, too, point out the religious orientation of primitive man: his awe and fear of the mysterious powers evidenced through nature and life; his recognition of the unseen sacred pervading the visible world, particularly potent in certain objects and at special times and places.

History merely puts on record tendencies of a remote, hidden past, coming down to us through myths, rites, and artifacts.

The classic writings of extant world religions and philosophies, the great religious books of the world, present to us the basic principles of their respective modes of mystical prayer. These writings have inspired countless volumes through the ages, commenting on and elaborating these principles. The *Vedas,* the ancient Hindu scriptures of unknown

71

authorship, are the direct source of Hinduism, and exercise considerable influence upon the other religions and philosophies of Asia. The *Upanishads,* the last of the four *Vedas,* contain philosophical and practical tenets characteristic of Oriental thought. The *Bhagavad-Gita,* another influential text, is part of a popular epic, the *Mahabharata,* deriving its substance from the *Vedas.* Hinduism is broad in its philosophical concepts, which are presented in mythological and ritualistic forms adaptable to uneducated people as well as to the educated. The most intellectual of the Hindu schools is the Vedanta, which still flourishes, not only in Asia but in many Western countries as well.

The essence of Hindu thought is that the multitudes of things and happenings we perceive are simply manifestations of the one ultimate reality, Brahman, beginningless, supreme, unthinkable. Although the Hindu sages have represented the various aspects of the One by innumerable gods and goddesses, these mythological figures are regarded as only reflections of the one ultimate reality, that Brahman himself is all the gods. Brahman as evidenced in the human being is called *Atman.* Atman, the individual, and Brahman, the ultimate, are one, are reality, the soul of the whole world. *Lila* is the activity of Brahman, his rhythmic, dynamic play in manifesting himself in the countless structures and happenings of the universe and then absorbing these forms again into himself. *Maya* is the illusion of believing these manifestations to be reality. *Karma* (action) is the active principle of the divine lila, the force of creation in a universe where all elements are connected with all others, since they are One. As long as persons are under the illusion of maya, they are in the bonds of karma and can be freed only when they profoundly realize the unity and harmony of all creation, including man, and order their lives accordingly. This may be achieved by *daily meditation* and various spiritual exercises aimed at bringing about liberation from maya and karma, and union with the supreme, impersonal One, Brahman. One favored method of liberation is *yoga* (to yoke, to join), exercises, physical and mental, designed to liberate individual souls and unite them with Brahman.

The founder of Buddhism, Siddhartha, an Indian prince and seer, retained the concepts of the one reality underlying all apparent creation, of maya, of karma, of nirvana (the state of union with the One). Brahman is called Dharmakaya, which pervades the material aspects of the universe. The Buddha bypassed the mythological and ritual elements of Hinduism, focusing on the psychological elements, especially liberation from suffering. Meditation and moderate ascetic practices, the assimilation of the four Noble Truths and the following of the Eightfold Path of self-development to buddhahood were directed toward the goal of the Awakening or Enlightenment.

Briefly, the Four Noble Truths are:

1. Life is dislocated; something has gone wrong.
2. The cause of this dislocation is that we are shut up within ourselves, separated from our brothers and sisters of the rest of the human race.
3. The cure of this dislocation is the overcoming of selfish craving.
4. This cure can be effected through the Eightfold Path.

The Eightfold Path includes the following considerations: right knowledge, right aspiration, right speech, right behavior, right livelihood, right effort, right mindfulness, right absorption. These eight concepts are springboards to expanded meditation and effort.

After the Buddha's death, two schools of his teaching emerged, the *Hinayana* and the *Mahayana*. The latter, the more flexible and assimilable of the two, spread across Asia, merging in China with Confucianism and especially Taoism, and in Japan developing as *Zen*.

Of the two principal philosophical and religious trends

73

in China, Confucianism was the more rational and practical, while Taoism was closer to nature, more intuitive and mystical. The essential features of Taoism were compatible with the Vedanta, with yoga, and with Mahayana Buddhism. The idea of liberation was strong, although for Lao-tzu, the founder, it was liberation from the rules of convention. An important insight is the element of constant change and transformation in nature, seen as the interplay between polar opposites *yin* and *yang* in a relationship that dynamically links the two. Examples of these opposites are dark and light, female and male, intuition and intellect, below and above, yielding and firm, rest and movement. Enlightenment occurs in passing beyond earthly opposites to their harmony in the One beyond. (In modern psychology, C. G. Jung and his school make much of the *union of opposites* in the development of the whole human person.) *Tao* (the Way) is the equivalent of Brahman and Dharmakaya. The keynote is spontaneous flow with nature to the state of perfect unity.

From a special type of Chinese spiritual discipline known as *Ch'an,* usually interpreted as meaning *meditation,* Zen developed. It is a blend of the Japanese temperament with Hindu and Buddhist mysticism, Taoist intimacy with nature and spontaneous flow, and Confucian practicality. Zen focuses exclusively on the Buddhist experience of enlightenment, which it calls *satori,* the immediate experience of the nature of all that exists, transcending all categories of thought and falling utterly short of human communication. Zen is not, however, a withdrawal from life but an alive engagement with everyday affairs. Emphasis is placed on meditation—in the proper setting with correct posture and breathing, body and mind disciplined into a harmonious unity. Deeply mystical, Zen suffuses daily living with mysticism: arrangement of house and garden, placing of flowers, painting, serving of tea, archery, human relationships.

Before moving in this sketch away from the mysticism of Asia to that of some other parts of the world, it might be well to draw attention to some aspects of the mysticism of the Far East that differ from that of the Near East and the West. The philosophical base of Oriental religions as a whole is monistic and pantheistic, and the underlying divine One is impersonal. In the Near East, for the most part, and in the West, philosophy and theology distinguish the Creator from his creation and the divine being is a personal God. Many elements of mystical prayer are the same in East and West; and many apparently fundamental disparities diminish when terms are carefully defined.

Although the great civilizations of Asia Minor, Northern Africa, and Eastern Europe have left us monuments, artifacts, myths of a religious nature, little so far can be deduced from our findings of the nature of the prayer of most of them. Israel, a relatively insignificant people in number, seems almost alone in carrying from this area into the present a considerable body of early writings shot through with mystical passages, especially in the books of the prophets and books of prayer and inspiration. Since this Jewish patrimony is part of the Christian heritage as well, it has exercised a powerful influence upon the Christian mysticism of the West. It is also one of the sources of Mohammedan mysticism. The keynote of the Jewish religion is to make holy: to make the earth holy, to make all details of the people's lives holy, to make a nation holy as God's people, chosen to keep alive among all mankind the knowledge of the holiness, goodness, and love of God. Their religion is one of joy and gratitude to God. Although their chief means of practicing their faith is in their exalted moral code and meaningful ritual, a deep life of personal prayer would be needed to maintain their ideals. From the earliest records of their history until the present, they have produced exemplars of mystical prayer.

Before continuing with the flowering of mysticism in the Judaeo-Christian evolvement, I would like to mention a few less well-known systems of spirituality that surely lent themselves to some contemplative prayer. Zoroaster of ancient Persia taught that the kingdom of God was within man, who was called to unite his will with that of God and struggle together with God against the powers of Evil until they would finally be subdued. Zoroastrianism has survived until our own times in the Parsis. A mystical element in the nature religion of the early North American Indians has persisted in the religious experiences of their descendants. Perhaps this is true of other primitive peoples, too. Because of subsequent effects upon Christianity, mention should also be briefly made of the Greek religious mysteries, of the various early Greek philosophers, especially Plato, and of the writings of Plotinus, whose Neoplatonic ideas deeply influenced early Christian writers on spirituality and prayer and who is considered by some the greatest philosopher of eclectic mysticism.

With regard to Jesus, we here can only touch upon the contemplative aspects of his life presented to us in the Gospels. Volumes have been, and will doubtless continue to be written, on his significant withdrawals from human contacts to wrestle with the darkness of his soul and to commune with his Father. First of all, we might note that the first thirty or so years of his life were spent in obscurity. He apparently did not attract attention to himself as a recluse, as John the Baptist did. But judging from the maturity of his teaching and ministry when he emerged as a public figure, these years must have been deeply grounded in the divine. Preceding his public life, there were the forty days and nights he spent in the desert, fasting and praying and wrestling with the powers of evil. We read in the Gospels of his withdrawing frequently into the mountains by himself to pray. Then also there is the significant event of the Transfiguration.

There are references in Jesus' teaching to sincere prayer from the heart, to avoiding long prayers in public but praying briefly in private. His words to the woman at the well in Samaria indicate the interiority desired of prayer: "But the hour is coming, and now is, when the true worshipers will worship the Father in spirit and truth" (John 4:23). Then again he spoke of love as the determining element: "If a man loves me, he will keep my word, and my Father will love him, and we will come to him and make our home with him"

(John 14:23). He promises to send the Holy Spirit: "And I will pray the Father, and he will give you another Counselor, to be with you forever, even the Spirit of truth" (John 14:16-17). Jesus faced the ordeal of his sufferings and death alone in the Garden of Gethsemane, grappling with his human agony and in this agony uniting his will with that of his Father.

The prayer of Jesus and his words on prayer point the way for Christian mysticism. Many times in process it has become entangled in cultures and historical movements. But its true direction has always seemed to survive in some individuals or schools and continues to evolve in our own time.

The descent of the Holy Spirit upon the first Christians is a vivid prototype of God's action in the mystical experience. St. Paul's conversion, his "awakening," is another example. He seems to have retired into the desert immediately afterward to work out with God the amazing insights given him. His epistles are filled with penetrating spiritual perceptions that could hardly have come to him except in intense meditation and mystical prayer. He describes an experience of being caught up into heaven and having had revealed to him what "eyes have not seen."

Many precepts for later developments of meditation and contemplation came from the early Fathers and Doctors of the Church. For the most part, their ideas were permeated by Neoplatonism, a philosophy that considered the material world the result of a fall from spirituality, which could be regained only by a transcending of the senses through mystical intuition.

Mystical prayer was cultivated by the Christian hermits of the third and fourth centuries and afterward chiefly in the monasteries and convents throughout the Middle Ages and later history. Various orders following the Benedictine Rule became famous for their contemplative life, notably the Cistercians, the Trappists, and the Carthusians. Among writers who affected the development of the mystical prayer of the West was Pseudo-Areopagite of the sixth century, an un-

77

known writer who used as a pen name Dionysius the Areopagite, the name of an Athenian judge of the first century who was converted to Christianity by St. Paul. One school of mysticism arose from the hermits living on Mount Carmel in Palestine. Gathered together under a common rule, they became known as the Order of Mount Carmel or Carmelites, and in the sixteenth century in Spain included in their number two of the most influential writers on Western mysticism, Teresa of Avila and John of the Cross. In the twelfth century, Francis of Assisi, a true mystic himself, became the spiritual father of a long line of contemplatives. And Dominic Guzman, founder of the Order of Preachers in the same century, emphasized contemplation in his life and rule, proposing as a motto to his friars, "Give to others of the fruits of your contemplation." Among Dominicans were such famous mystics as Catherine of Siena, Johannes Eckhart, called the founder of German mysticism, and his disciple Johannes Tauler, who fostered the contemplative prayer of the widespread lay movement known as the Friends of God. Another well-known mystic of the German school was the Fleming Jan Ruysbroeck, whose hermitage near Brussels was for thirty-eight years a center of pilgrimage for those seeking instruction in the mystical life. There Ruysbroeck communed with nature, contemplated, counseled pilgrims, and wrote a series of books that rank high among mystical treatises.

We have spoken of the Italian mystics, the German mystics, the Spanish mystics. Each country of Europe has its group, often with the same early roots, often influencing each other, but each manifesting native tendencies. Among the English mystics are the famous four: Richard Rolle, Lady Julian of Norwich, Walter Hilton, and the author of *The Cloud of Unknowing,* each of whose works has found a place not only in mysticism but in English literature as well. In medieval France there are among others St. Bernard and Clairvaux and the school of St. Victor in Paris. There are Sweden with its St. Brigid and Russia with its Mount Athos and its "Prayer of Jesus": "Lord Jesus Christ, Son of God, have mercy on me, a sinner." Beyond Europe in the later Near East and Africa, we have the Muslim Sufi.

Not only did the ancient West and the Middle Ages flourish in mystical development, but each succeeding century adds its contribution. Only to touch on a few instances of the last three centuries, there come quickly to mind Jacob Boehme, the remarkable Lutheran shoemaker mystic; Pascal and the Port Royal school; Brother Lawrence with his simple formula of the presence of God; Margaret Mary Alacoque with her devotion to the Sacred Heart of Jesus, and the Quakers, all of the seventeenth century; William Blake, the mystic poet, and Paul of the Cross, founder of the Passionist Order, of the eighteenth century; the Cure of Ars, a simple parish priest whose union with God made him a light for souls; Charles de Foucauld, mystic of the Sahara; Therese of Lisieux and Elizabeth of the Trinity, French Carmelite nuns whose lives and teaching inspired many to contemplative prayer, as examples from the nineteenth century; Father Doyle, chaplain in World War I, who repeated short prayers almost continuous on the battlefield of Europe; Edith Stein, Jewish Carmelite mystic martyred by Nazis; Thomas Merton, well-known American Trappist contemplative and author; the French Protestant center for prayer at Taizé, and the charismatic movements of the twentieth century.

In the East, monasteries and renowned masters flourished also during these centuries. Scholars researched the ancient books and wrote commentaries on them. Eventually interchange between East and West became acceptable. Among the many oriental masters who, in the last two centuries, have written in English or been translated into English, are S.N. Dasgupta, author of *Hindu Mysticism* and other books and articles; Sri Ramakrishna, renowned master whose teachings have been translated; Swami Vivekananda, prolific writer and lecturer; Rājendralāla Mitra, author of *Buddha Gayā, the Hermitage of Sākya Muni* and editor and translator of *The Yoga Aphorisms of Patanjali, with the Commentary of Bhoja Rāja;* Ananda Coomaraswamy, author of *Buddha and the*

79

Gospel of Buddhism and other books; D. T. Suzuki, influential Zen scholar; and Eknath Easwaran, contemporary lecturer and recent commentator on a series of books on the *Bhagavad-Gita.*

Both Eastern and Western mystics show us that, in part, communion with the divine is an art. There is a discipline on our side to prepare a space, a readiness, for God's part: the Enlightenment, the act of union, or whatever the mystical experience might be. Solitude, quiet, and concentration are demanded, and this atmosphere calls for the discipline of arranging for the right environment and training ourselves to persevere in it. Control of sleep and a simple diet are part of the discipline in both East and West. In contrast with the idea that discipline is a punishment for sin, it is seen here as the *freeing* of the faculties for greater good. Submission to a master or teacher seems a more important element of discipline in the East than in the West, at least the West of modern times, where in most instances the focus is upon each of us discovering his/her own individual genius for prayer and the circumstances that can best foster it.

A significant element in the process of meditation for the Hindu and the Mahayana Buddhist is the *mantra,* a sacred sound, word, or verse, which is repeated over and over to free the soul. The syllable *om* is considered a sacred sound and is most frequently chosen. The Zen Buddhist uses the *koan,* a problem that cannot be solved by the intellect alone, to liberate the meditation from reasoning (see "A Note on the Koan" at the end of this appendix). The repetition of some short invocation, like the Prayer of Jesus of the Russians, is sometimes employed in the West, but usually reflective meditation is the prelude to the goal: contemplation, the direct experience of God. For both the East and the West, the end of meditation is the immediate experience of the transcendent, although Westerners travel a longer time by way of the intellect first, a route Orientals strive to eliminate immediately.

Two approaches to prayer are evident in both Eastern

and Western religions: the dark and the light, the negative and the positive, the road of suffering and the road of joy, or, for the Christian, the way of the Crucifixion or of the Resurrection. Different temperaments have affinities for different modes. People who have endured much pain and trouble tend to concentrate on suffering. The Buddha set himself to eradicate suffering. Through the hardships of the early Middle Ages, the Crucifixion was a meaningful Christian approach to God. In Italy, Spain, and parts of the Near East, among the Celtic monks and certain German mystics, excessive practices of bodily laceration in empathy with the crucified Lord prevailed. Emphasis on the sinfulness of man and the justice of God exacerbated these customs.

In some parts of the Near East the Resurrection was highlighted. Among most of the German and English mystics, simplicity, peace, trust, and joy prevailed; and scattered throughout Europe, holy persons focusing on the God of Love radiated a luminous tranquillity and happiness. Whether union is sought with an impersonal One or a personal God of Love makes a difference, also. It seems almost as if the joy and serenity of the Eastern mystic evinces a sense of escape from the illusions and sufferings of this life, as contrasted with the active delights of union with a personal God. However, if the personal God is conceived solely as a God of Power, judging and punishing, it is hard to imagine a mystical relationship with him.

A Note on the Koan

An example of the koan is: "You can hear the sound of two hands clapped together. What is the sound of one hand clapping?" A story is told of a disciple who reported to the master each evening the solution to this koan he had arrived at during the day. All of his answers—the music of the geishas, the sound of dripping water, the sighing of the wind, the cry of an owl, the song of the locusts, and so on—received a negative response. After a year of exploring all the sounds of his environment and pondering over them, he finally entered into true meditation, transcended all sounds, and reached soundless sound.

Other examples are:

"What was the appearance of your face before your ancestors were born?"

"A cow passes by a window. Its head, horns, and four legs all pass by. Why did not the tail pass by?"

It is not the answer that is important, but the process.

Jesus often used this device. Recall his words to Nicodemus: "Unless one is born anew, he cannot see the kingdom of God." Nicodemus was puzzled: "How can a man be born when he is old? Can he enter a second time into his mother's womb and be born?" (John 3:3–4).

Or consider Jesus' encounter with the woman by the well in Samaria. He stirred up her curiosity by the statement: "Every one who drinks of this water will thirst again, but whoever drinks of the water that I shall give him will never thirst" (John 4:13).

Some other examples from the Gospels are: "many that are first will be last and the last first" (Mark: 10:31); "whoever would save his life will lose it, and whoever loses his life for my sake will save it" (Luke 9:24); "For as Jonah was three days and three nights in the belly of the whale, so will the Son of Man be three days and three nights in the heart of the earth" (Matthew 12:40).

For more about koans, refer to *The Religions of Man* by Huston Smith (New York: Harper and Row, 1958), Perennial Library Edition, pages 146–149; and to *The Gospel According to Zen,* edited by Robert Sohl and Audrey Carr. (New York: New American Library, 1970), pages 71–78.

Notes

Chapter 1

1. Among the poets who have the power to raise one's consciousness of God speaking through nature, I would especially recommend Gerard Manley Hopkins. Some of the Psalms, also, emphasize God in nature.

Among prose writers, I would mention especially Pierre Teilhard de Chardin, notably his *Hymn of the Universe*.

Bernard Basset, S.J., *Let's Start Praying Again* (New York: Herder and Herder, 1972) proposes reading books on science rather than "devotional" books as preparation for prayer.

Chapter 2

1. *The Oxford Annotated Bible*. Revised Standard Version (New York: Oxford University Press, 1965), Genesis 1:26–28. Italics mine. This version of the Bible has been used for all quotations in this book.
2. Genesis 2:15.
3. Genesis 1:31.
4. Matthew 25:35–45.
5. Matthew 18:20.

Chapter 3

A few good books for background reading for this chapter would be:

Pierre Teilhard de Chardin, *The Phenomenon of Man* (New York: Harper and Row, 1959).

Abraham H. Maslow, *Toward a Psychology of Being* (New York: D. Van Nostrand, 1968).

C. G. Jung, *Modern Man in Search of a Soul* (New York: Harcourt, Brace, and World, 1933), especially Chapter 9, "The Basic Postulates of Analytical Psychology."

Matthew Fox, *Whee! We, Wee All the Way Home* (Consortium, 1976).

Chapter 4

1. Matthew 6:6.

Chapter 5

1. Genesis 32:24–30.
2. Among studies supporting this statement, I would include the following:

Mircea Eliade, *The Sacred and the Profane* (New York: Harper and Row, 1961).
William James, *The Varieties of Religious Experience* (New York: The New American Library, 1958).
C. G. Jung, *Two Essays on Analytical Psychology* (New York: Meridian Books, 1953).
————, *Modern Man in Search of a Soul* (New York: Harcourt, Brace, and World, 1933), see the chapters "Archaic Man" and "The Basic Postulates of Analytical Psychology."
Pierre Teilhard de Chardin, *The Phenomenon of Man* (New York: Harper and Row, 1961), especially Book Three, Chapter II 4, "The Neolithic Metamorphosis," to the end.
3. Simone Weil, *Waiting for God* (New York: G. P. Putnam's Sons, 1951), p. 69.
4. Genesis 1:28; 2:5.
5. Mircea Eliade, *The Sacred and the Profane.*
6. Matthew 7:16–20.

Chapter 6

1. Vatican II, *Dogmatic Constitution on Divine Revelation,* 21.
2. Barnabas Ahern, *The Formation of Scripture* (Chicago: Argus Communications, 1967).
3. Some important books by biblical scholars:

William F. Albright, *From the Stone Age to Christianity* (New York: Doubleday, 1957).
Raymond E. Brown, S.S., Joseph A. Fitzmyer, S.J., Roland E. Murphy, O. Carm., Editors, *The Jerome Biblical Commentary* (Englewood, N.J.: Prentice-Hall, 1968).
Herbert F. Hahn, *The Old Testament in Modern Research* (Philadelphia: Fortress Press, 1966).
R. K. Harrison, *The Dead Sea Scrolls* (N.Y.: Harper, 1961).

John L. McKenzie, *Dictionary of the Bible* (New York: Macmillan, 1965).
————, *The Two-Edged Sword* (Milwaukee: Bruce, 1956).
Bruce Vawter, *On Genesis: A New Reading* (New York: Doubleday, 1977) This book supersedes Vawter's *A Path Through Genesis* (New York: Sheed and Ward, 1956), a much smaller book and an exciting introduction to the ways of modern biblical scholarship.
4. Vatican II, *Dogmatic Constitution on Divine Revelation*, 25. The inner quote is from St. Ambrose, fourth century Doctor of the Church.
5. Another example, Bernard Bassett, S.J., *Let's Start Praying Again* (New York: Herder and Herder, 1972).
6. The entire poem is included in the revised breviary, *Christian Prayer: The Liturgy of the Hours*, Appendix: Poetry (New York: The Catholic Book Publishing Co., 1976). In the one-volume edition, pp. 2059–60.
7. Gerard Manley Hopkins, "God's Grandeur."
8. T. S. Eliot, *The Waste Land*, 11. 61–63.
9. Ibid., 11. 15–16.
10. Ibid., 1. 126.
11. T. S. Eliot, "The Love Song of J. Alfred Prufrock."
12. T. S. Eliot, "Gerontion."
13. Gerard Manley Hopkins, "Thou Art Indeed Just, Lord."
14. W. H. Auden, "Petition."
15. Leslie Brandt, *Psalms/Now* (St. Louis: Concordia, 1973).
16. Moses, in Exodus 15:1–4, 8–13, 17–18; Deuteronomy 2:2–5; 12:1–6; 26:1–4, 7–9, 12; 32; 33:13–16; 38:10–14, 17–20; 40:10–17; 42:10–16; 61:10–62:5; 66:10–14; Anna, in 1 Samuel 2:1–10; Sirach, in Ecclesiasticus; Isaiah 45:15–25; Hezekiah, Isaiah 39:10–20; Jeremiah 14:17–21; 31:10–14; The Three Young Men, in Daniel 3, parts of 26–88; Habakkuk 3:2–4, 13, 15–19; Tobit 13:1–8, 8–11, 13–15; Judith 16:2–3, 13–15.
17. John Frederick Nims (translator), *The Poems of St. John of the Cross* (New York: Grove Press, 1959), "The Spiritual Canticle," p. 3, stanzas 1, 2, and 4.
18. Luke 1:68–79.
19. Luke 1:46–55.
20. 1 Samuel 2:1–10.
21. Luke 2:29–32.
22. Mark 9:22–26.
23. Mark 10:51.
24. Matthew 8.

Chapter 7

1. Carl Jung, ed., *Man and His Symbols* (New York: Dell, 1964) 57.
2. Aniela Jaffé in *Jung, Man and His Symbols*, pp. 257 ff. Specific mention is made of the stone Jacob set up and anointed after his dream of the ladder reaching to heaven. Also, the stone circle at Stonehenge. Attention is drawn to the lion, ox, and eagle used as symbols for the evangelists Mark, Luke, and John.

3. Ibid., p. 75.

4. Mircea Eliade, *The Sacred and the Profane* (New York.: Harper and Row, 1959).

5. Suzanne K. Langer, *Philosophy in a New Key* (New York: New American Library, 1948), p. 42.

6. Ibid., p. 52.

7. Ibid., p. 46.

8. Ibid., p. 45.

9. Ibid., pp. 42–52.

10. Jung, *Man and His Symbols,* pp. 41–42.

11. Matthew 25:40.

12. Vatican Council II, *The Constitution on the Sacred Liturgy* (1963), 14.

13. Ibid., 21.

14. John 14:6.

15. *The Constitution on the Sacred Liturgy,* 83–101. The approved English version of the revised breviary is called *Christian Prayer,* The Liturgy of the Hours (New York: Catholic Book Publishing Co., 1976).

16. *Constitution on the Sacred Liturgy,* 47.

17. Ibid., 24.

18. Sister M. Laurentia Digges, CSJ, *Transfigured World* (New York: Farrar, Strauss, and Cudahy, 1957), p. 70.

19. The work recently done in developing a new set of symbols for the funeral mass may indicate what may be done. Father Nolan (see Bibliography) describes it this way: "With the funeral mass (where to the mystification of some we still use the word celebrate), the church has been developing a new set of signs. Those who are still in the 'days of wrath' (*Dies irae*) might not know that the Paschal candle is now used to lead the procession, Easter songs are sung, bright vestments worn, and a festive pall with a sign of faith or peace is lowered over the coffin."

20. Daniel Callahan, "Putting the Liturgy in Its Place," *National Catholic Reporter,* August 9, 1967.

21. Isaiah 1:13-17. Italics mine.

22. Among such authors is Daniel Callahan, whose article cited above is most thought-provoking. He develops his thesis that "we cease placing the liturgy at the top of our table of Christian values. The liturgy undeniably belongs in our table of Christian values, but not at the top and very possibly not even near the top.

"Much more important are love of neighbor, service to the world, the sharing of each other's burdens, and a sense of responsibility for man and nature."

23. "The Church as a Ministering Community," brochure for The 1977 Liturgical Week, August 8–11, Iowa City, Iowa. Sponsored by The Liturgical Conference.

Selected Bibliography

When I first started thinking about this book, I did not know of a single volume on prayer I would want to suggest to a friend who asked me, "How do you pray?" Since I started writing it, however, I have come across two books, which, had I known of their existence, would have deterred me from undertaking this project. From different points of view they have said what I have said and more, and have said it wittily. There might be a statement here or there I wouldn't go along with. But as I read these books, I glowed with a feeling of kinship with their authors and recognized what I myself had experienced and felt deeply about. I proudly recommend *On Becoming a Musical, Mystical Bear* by Matthew Fox, and *Let's Start Praying Again* by Bernard Basset, S.J. The first has as subtitle "Spirituality American Style," and the second, "Field Work in Meditation."

Books come into style and go out of style. Language changes, and metaphors lose their significance. But if I were to draw up a reading list right now for an inquirer about prayer, this is what I think I would do. I would place *my* little volume first as an introduction, as a sort of general map of the world of prayer. Then I would suggest Bernard Basset's *Let's Start Praying Again,* to be followed by Matthew Fox's *On Becoming a Musical, Mystical Bear.* These would be the jumping-off points and the guidelines for the adventurer into the spiritual world.

Before finishing these three books, my enquirer would have commenced exploring the Bible for its "purple patches" of inspiration. Prayer would have begun. And after a bit of the "field work" proposed by Father Basset, I would lead my seeker after prayer to other modern masters for stimulation and impetus. Morton Kelsey's *The Other Side of Silence* would be an early choice. Henri J. M. Nouwen's *Reaching Out* would be helpful, especially chapter 7, "Prayer and Mortality," and chapter 8, "The Prayer of the Heart." Perhaps *Practical Mysticism* by Evelyn Underhill would be enlightening.

If scriptural prayer has been progressing all this while, the enquirer may be ready for *The Divine Milieu* by Pierre Teilhard de Chardin. This is a work not for reading only but for meditating on. It needs slow perusal and absorption in prayer.

I would advise alternating periods of scriptural prayer with reflective meditation on modern works, such as Morton Kelsey's book, already mentioned, especially Part Five, Thomas Merton's *Seeds of Contemplation,* Henri Nouwen's *Reaching Out,* William Callahan and Francine Cardman's *The Wind Is Rising*, and Teilhard's *The Divine Milieu.*

Father Basset's remarks on *reading, thinking,* and *praying* in chapter 6 of *Let's Start Praying Again* are worth considering in the selection of books for prayer. God can, of course, directly spark the core of our being with the fire for prayer, but he rarely chooses to do so. Normally, prayer is kindled by reading, hearing, or experiencing immediately some insight through the senses or emotions. These triggers to prayer should be chosen with a view to heightening perception and awareness.

Basset quotes Thomas More in referring to books that lead to God and books that do not. Any book that leads to God is acceptable; it does not need to be in the category of "spiritual" books. It may be science, travel, biography, poetry, drama, reflection. Hammarskjöld's *Markings,* Anne Lindbergh's *Gifts of the Sea,* Bach's *Jonathan Livingston Seagull,* Capra's *The Tao of Physics,* Bronowski's *The Ascent of Man* may set prayer off as readily as the works of John of the Cross.

A passage of Paul to the Romans quoted by Basset points this out: "How deep is the mine of God's wisdom, of his knowledge . . ."

In selecting books for meditation, then, we do well to enlarge the circle of our reading, not in a desultory way, but in view of fixing our attention on the height, the depth, the breadth of the wonder of our God. Nothing that is of truth is foreign to him.

For the most part, the works I have been mentioning in this portion of my book are those of modern authors. Once the inquirer has achieved an overview of the spiritual life and has grasped the relevance and desirability of personally becoming a person of prayer of the twentieth century, a knowledge of the spiritual classics of ages past will be alluring. Most of these have been touched upon in the appendix, "A Sketch of the History of Mysticism," and will be included in the list of books at the end of this section. It is important to evaluate these writings in view of the times and cultures from which they have sprung. While extremely worthwhile as testimonies of the genuineness of a mystical tendency in human beings of all ages and as sources of inspiration and insight, they may not be completely applicable to the prayer needs of our particular point in evolution.

If the seeker after a spiritual life has not been able to *let go* in reflective meditation on Holy Scriptures or other prayerful writings, perhaps *Prayers* by Michel Quoist would give the feeling of how it can be done. In these prayers, things, events, and people of the daily, contemporary scene rebound against passages of Scripture in a way meaningful to modern human experience. Some paraphrases of parts of the Bible, such as *Epistles/Now* and *Psalms/Now* by Leslie Brandt might provide insights as to how the joys and sufferings of our own age and culture find themselves in a Scriptural context.

In general then, some of the books that I have found helpful in stimulating my prayer are listed below:

Some Helpful Books for Growth
In Prayer and the Spiritual Life

Albright, William Foxwell, *From the Stone Age to Christianity*. New York: Doubleday. First published by the Johns Hopkins Press, 1940.

Bailey, Raymond, *Thomas Merton on Mysticism*. New York: Doubleday, 1975.

Basset, Bernard, S.J., *Let's Start Praying Again*. New York: Herder and Herder, 1972.

Baum, Gregory, ed., *Journeys*. New York: Paulist, 1975.

Brandt, Leslie, *Epistles/Now*. St. Louis: Concordia, 1974.

————, *Psalms/Now*. St. Louis: Concordia, 1973.

————, *Jesus/Now*. St. Louis: Concordia, 1978.

————, *Prophets/Now*. St. Louis: Concordia, 1979.

Buber, Martin, *I and Thou*. New York, Scribner's Sons, 1958.

Callahan, William, S.J., and Francine Cardman, editors. *The Wind Is Rising*. Hyattsville, Md.: Quixote Center, 1978.

Capra, Fritjof, *The Tao of Physics*. Berkeley: Shambhala, 1975.

Chapman, Dom John, O.S.B., *Spiritual Letters,* edited by Dom Roger Hudleston. London: Sheed and Ward, 1938.

Cheney, Sheldon, *Men Who Have Walked With God*. New York: Alfred A. Knopf, 1945.

Digges, Sister M. Laurentia, C.S.J., *Transfigured World*. New York: Farrar, Straus and Cudahy, 1957.

Eliade, Mircea, *The Sacred and the Profane*. New York: Harper & Row, 1957.

Eliot, T. S., *The Complete Poems and Plays*. New York: Harcourt, Brace, and World, c. 1930-1962.

Fox, Matthew, O.P., *On Becoming a Musical, Mystical Bear*. New York: Paulist, 1972.

Hammarskjöld, Dag, *Markings*. New York: Alfred A. Knopf, 1966.

Hopkins, Gerard Manley, *Poems and Prose*. Baltimore: Penguin, 1953.

James, William, *The Varieties of Religious Experience*. New York: New American Library, 1958.

Johnston, William, *Christian Zen*. New York: Harper & Row, 1971.

————, *The Still Point: Reflections of Zen and Christian Mysticism*. New York: Harper & Row, 1970.

Jung, Carl, *Man and His Symbols*. New York: Dell, 1968.

————, *Modern Man in Search of a Soul*. New York: Harcourt, Brace & World, 1933.

Kelsey, Morton, *The Other Side of Silence*. New York: Paulist, 1976.

Langer, Susanne, *Philosophy in a New Key*. New York: New American Library, 1942.

Maslow, Abraham, *Toward a Psychology of Being*. New York: D. Van Nostrand, 1968.

McKenzie, John L., *The Two-edged Sword*. Milwaukee: Bruce, 1956.

Merton, Thomas, *Contemplation in a World of Action*. New York.: Doubleday, 1971.

————, *New Seeds of Contemplation.* New York: New Directions, 1961.
————, *No Man Is an Island.* New York: Harcourt, Brace, 1955.
————, *Seeds of Contemplation.* New York: New Directions, 1949.
Nouwen, Henri J.M., *Reaching Out,* New York: Doubleday, 1975.
Quoist, Michel, *Prayers,* New York: Sheed and Ward, 1963.
Rogers, Carl, *On Becoming a Person.* Boston: Houghton Mifflin, 1961.
Smith, Huston, *The Religions of Man.* New York: Harper & Row, 1958.
Teilhard de Chardin, Pierre, *The Divine Milieu.* New York.: Harper & Row, 1960.
————, *Hymn of the Universe.* New York: Harper & Row, 1965.
Thérèse, Saint, *Autobiography of St. Thérèse of Lisieux.* New York: P. J. Kenedy and Sons, 1958.
Underhill, Evelyn, *Mysticism.* New York: Dutton, 1911.
————, *Practical Mysticism.* New York: Dutton, 1915.
Vawter, Bruce, *A Path Through Genesis,* New York: Sheed and Ward, 1956.
————, *On Genesis: A New Reading.* New York: Doubleday, 1977.
Weil, Simone, *Waiting for God.* New York: Putnam, 1951.

Some Other Background and Complementary Reading for Understanding the Spiritual Life

Bronowski, J., *The Ascent of Man.* Boston: Little Brown, 1973.
————, *The Cloud of Unknowing.* Translated by Ira Progoff. New York: Julian Press, 1957.
Coomaraswamy, Ananda, *Buddha and the Gospel of Buddhism.* New York: University Books, 1964.
Dasgupta, S. N., *Hindu Mysticism.* Chicago and London, 1927.
The Documents of Vatican II, New York: Guild Press, 1966.
Eliade, Mircea, *Yoga.* Princeton University Press, 1958.
Easwaren, Eknath, *The Bhagavad Gita for Daily Living.* Berkeley: The Blue Mountain Center of Meditation, 1975.
————, *Meditation.* Petaluma: Nilgiri Press, 1978.
Eckhart, Johannes, *Meister Eckhart: Mystic and Philosopher.* Bloomington: Indiana University Press, 1978.
Evely, Louis, *Our Prayer.* New York: Herder and Herder, 1970.
————, *Teach Us How to Pray.* New York: Newman Press, 1967.
Fox, Matthew, O.P., *Whee! We, Wee All the Way Home.* Consortium, 1976.
Graham, Aelred, O.S.B., *The Love of God.* New York.: Doubleday, 1959.
Happold, F. C., *Prayer and Meditation.* Baltimore: Penguin, 1971.
Higgins, John J., S.J., *Thomas Merton on Prayer.* New York: Doubleday, 1975.
John of the Cross, *The Collected Works of St. John of the Cross.* Translated by Kieran Kavanaugh and Otilio Rodríguez. New York: Doubleday, 1964.

Jung, Carl, *Two Essays on Analytical Psychology*. New York: World, 1953.
Kierkegaard, Soren, *Fear and Trembling*. Translated by Walter Lowrie. Princeton: Princeton University Press, 1941.
Lawrence, Brother, *The Practice of the Presence of God*. New York: Revell, 1895.
Lockyer, Herbert, *All the Prayers of the Bible*. Grand Rapids: Zondervan Publishing House, 1959.
Lubac, Henri de, S.J., *The Religion of Teilhard de Chardin*. New York: Doubleday, 1968.
Merton, Thomas, *The Asian Journal of Thomas Merton*. New York: New Directions, 1973.
————, *Contemplative Prayer*. New York: Herder and Herder, 1969.
————, *Mystics and Zen Masters*. New York: Dell, 1961.
————, *Thoughts in Solitude*. New York: Farrar, Straus & Cudahy, 1956.
Nolan, Joseph T., "Liturgy Is One Way of Teaching." *National Catholic Reporter*. October 27, 1972.
Prabhavananda, Swami, *Spiritual Heritage of India*. Hollywood: The Vedanta Society, 1964.
————, *The Sermon on the Mount according to Vedanta*. Hollywood: The Vedanta Society, 1964.
Rahner, Karl, *On Prayer*. New York: Paulist, 1968.
Suzuki, D. T., *Essays in Zen Buddhism*. London: Rider, 1927, 1950, 1958.
————, *Introduction to Zen Buddhism*. London, 1960.
Tanquerey, Adolphe. S.J., *The Spiritual Life*.
The Book of Tao. Translation by Frank MacHovec. New York: Peter Pauper Press, 1962.
St. Teresa of Avila. *The Autobiography of St. Teresa of Avila*. New York: Doubleday, 1960.
————, *The Interior Castle*. New York: Doubleday, 1961.
————, *The Way of Perfection*. Westminster, Md.: Newman, 1961.
Teilhard de Chardin, Pierre. *The Phenomenon of Man*. New York: Harper, 1959.
Thomas à Kempis. *The Imitation of Christ*. New York: Sheed and Ward, 1959.
The Upanishads. Translated by Swami Prabhavananda and Frederick Manchester. New York: New American Library, 1957.
Vivekananda, Swami. *Jñāna-Yoga*. New York: Ramakrishna-Vivekananda Center, 1970.
————, *Karma-Yoga*. Calcutta: Advaita Ashrama, 1963.